Professional Dining Room Management

CAROL A. KING

HAYDEN BOOK COMPANY, INC.
Rochelle Park, New Jersey

Library of Congress Cataloging in Publication Data

King, Carol A.
  Professional dining room management.

  Bibliography: p.
  Includes index.
  1. Restaurant management. I. Title.
TX911.3.M27K56   647'.95'068   80-15228
ISBN 0-8104-9471-X

1	2	3	4	5	6	7	8	9	PRINTING
80	81	82	83	84	85	86	87	88	YEAR

Preface

This book is written for the forgotten men and women of the restaurant business—the first line supervisors, specifically those who oversee the service function of the business. Many books, films, and training materials are available that deal with technical aspects of the business: how to wait table, serve wine, mix drinks, and other aspects of food preparation, as well as management tasks such as accounting, budgeting, marketing, purchasing, personnel management, and administration. However, few materials are available to assist the supervisor whose staff must meet and serve the public.

The service supervisor's job is a key one in the restaurant business since a large part of the guest's dining experience and satisfaction is derived from the interpersonal contact between guest and staff. If this contact is not satisfactory, all the care and investment in decor, food selection, and preparation are for naught.

Some of the material presented here was first developed for Harris Kerr Forster & Co.'s book *Profitable Food and Beverage Management: Operations* by Eric Green, Galen Drake, and Jerome Sweeney (Hayden Book Company, Inc., 1978). For readers seeking a general text on food and beverage operations, that book and its companion volume, *Profitable Food and Beverage Management: Planning,* are recommended.

I wish to thank Eric Green and the partners of Harris, Kerr, Forster & Co. for permission to use their material in this volume. I would also like to thank Tony Aigner, Alan Lewis, and Dennis Sweeney for permission to include illustrative material from Windows on the World, The Market Bar and Dining Rooms, and The Corner restaurants.

The English language is a bit cumbersome when it comes to masculine and feminine pronouns. Rather than burden the reader with he/she and waiter/waitress throughout the text, we have used the masculine form.

Contents

Chapter 1

Introduction

In most dining room operations, the ultimate objective is to make a profit, both this year and in the long run. There are some types of table service operations, such as private clubs or executive dining rooms, where the primary objective is to give service to the patron. However, even in a nonprofit situation, the goal is to provide the best possible service for the amount of money spent. There are few, if any, nonprofit organizations these days that can afford to let their operating costs run out of control.

Remember that the objective in commercial restaurants is to remain profitable in the long run. Anyone can make a fast buck by bleeding the business and gypping the customer. To remain profitable a restaurant must offer good value to its customers and job satisfaction to its employees and managers. Why job satisfaction? Well, profits are made by people. Having a stable, trained, and motivated staff certainly makes the job easier.

Good value to the customer does not mean cheap prices. It refers to the quality and quantity of food, the level of service, and the decor and ambiance provided for the price paid. There are few real bargains in this world, but the enterprising manager who can offer more to his customers than the competitor down the street will do well.

Good service is one of the primary things people consider in judging value in a restaurant. While good service cannot overcome problems of poor quality food or sloppy housekeeping, poor service can ruin an otherwise excellent meal for the guest and cost the restaurant considerable goodwill and repeat business.

Regardless of the type of restaurant, good service always has two requirements: efficiency and courtesy. Efficient service doesn't necessarily mean speed. Rather, it means serving each course at the right time, with the food at the proper temperature and with all the required accompaniments and utensils. In a coffee shop, efficient service is fast

1

service; in a luxury restaurant, it is service that is timed to allow the guest to enjoy a liesurely meal, with each course served exactly when he is ready for it.

A pleasant, courteous staff can make a strong contribution to the restaurant's overall public image. If the personnel are genuinely interested in providing good service, guests will leave with good feelings about their dining experience.

The restaurant business is a people business, and running a dining room is a lot more than just bringing in the food and carrying out the dishes. It is really the business of satisfying people's needs—a complicated and demanding profession.

The needs people seek to satisfy when dining out go far beyond basic satisfaction of hunger. They are often looking for status or ego satisfaction, recognition, new experiences, excitement, entertainment, acceptance, and welcome. In fact, the quality of the human relationship is often valued far more than the quality of the food or the decor of the dining room.

Therefore, the first requirement of a good service employee is a customer-oriented attitude, that is, a genuine desire to please the guest. This attitude recognizes that the guest is the reason for being in business and the source of everyone's paychecks. It is not an attitude of demeaning servitude, but rather one of professional hospitality.

The title of this book is *Professional Dining Room Management*. What does it mean to be a professional in this business? First, of course, it means mastering the skills of one's calling. But being a professional goes beyond learning a set of skills. It means

- Having a commitment to the highest standard of performance at all times
- Having a dedication to one's career and putting the interests of the job first
- Keeping up with new ideas and trends in the industry
- Continuing one's education by taking courses, reading books and trade magazines, and visiting other restaurants to see what they are doing
- Helping others develop their skills and guiding young people in planning their careers
- Joining professional organizations and working with others in the field for the good of the industry

How does a dining room manager achieve a professional level of service in his dining room? Good service is not an accident; it doesn't just happen. It is the result of planning, organization, and supervision. The dining room manager needs four kinds of skills to achieve it.

1. He must be a good technician; that is, he knows the mechanics of serving food.
2. He must be a good supervisor—directing, training, and motivating his staff.
3. He must be a good front man—able to meet the public and merchandise his restaurant while promoting sales.
4. He must be a good manager—organizing the work flow and controlling costs in his department.

This book provides a guide for achieving professional service in the dining room, whether it is a coffee shop or a luxury restaurant. Since there are a number of books available on the technical aspects of service, this book stresses the management and supervisory aspects. In Appendix D (p. 149) you will find a number of good technical books on service.

Chapter 2

Types of Dining Room Service

Three types of service are commonly used in restaurants in the United States: French, Russian, and American. Other types are sometimes used, such as buffet service for special occasions and parties, family style, and tray service.

French Service

This style of service is found in restaurants offering classic French cuisine and in other types of operations that cater to a sophisticated clientele (see Fig. 2.1).

French service is distinguished by the fact that all or part of the preparation of the dish, or at least the finishing, is done in the dining room. The food is brought from the kitchen on silver platters, carefully arranged and suitably garnished, and presented to the guest for his inspection. The captain or maître d' then completes the preparation on a cart or *guéridon* next to the guest's table. A *rechaud* or alcohol lamp may be used for warming or for last minute sautéing of an item. This finishing is done in the guest's presence and to his exact preference. If offers him not only personalized attention, but also a show, depending on the skill and personality of the staff.

A highly skilled staff is required to give good French service. A captain must know how to bone fish and poultry, carve meats, dress salads, and prepare flaming and chafing dish items. Waiters must be familiar with the ingredients and methods for preparing numerous classic dishes, and busboys must be trained in the proper serving techniques.

Unfortunately, many operators attempt to offer French service without having a properly trained staff, resulting in service that is a poor imitation at best. It lacks one of the prime ingredients that gives French service its dignity—namely, professionalism. Each detail of true French service is done in consideration of the guest and is not a pointless empty ritual.

French service is very expensive if executed properly and requires a high menu price. A large staff of skilled waiters, captains, and bus help is

Fig. 2.1. French service. The waiter prepares medallions of beef on the gueridon at the guests' tableside. (*Courtesy* of The Four Seasons, New York City.)

required. A large inventory of hollow ware must be bought and maintained, as well as a large quantity of flatware, china, and high quality glassware. Because of the numerous pieces of ware required for the service of each guest, warewashing can also be a major expense. Furthermore, since side tables are required for French service, fewer dining tables can be placed in a given area. French service should not be rushed; usually only one seating can be obtained for each meal. All of these requirements limit the potential sales that can be obtained in a given space.

Russian Service

Service a la Russe, or Russian service, is a variation of French service (see Fig. 2.2). The major difference is that in Russian service, all carving and finishing is done in the kitchen. The individual portions are then arranged on trays or platters and garnished attractively. The waiter

Fig. 2.2. Russian service. The veal cutlet has been arranged on the platter and garnished in the kitchen. (*Courtesy* of The Four Seasons, New York City.)

carries the tray directly to the table and, after presenting it for inspection, serves the food onto the empty plate before the guest. The advantage of Russian service is that hot food does not get cold while it is being finished in the dining room. This service is most often used for banquets where all the guests are being served at the same time.

Fig. 2.3. American or plate service. The food has been arranged on the plate in the kitchen and is presented to the guest by the waiter.

American Service

In American service all food is plated and garnished in the kitchen. The filled plates are then carried to the dining room and placed before the guest (see Fig. 2.3). There are many advantages to this type of service, which accounts for its widespread use. The highly skilled French service waiter and captain are not required. Plating and garnishing can be done under the supervision of the chef, and an attractive arrangement of the items and garnishes can be devised. Finally, the food is more likely to be the proper temperature when it is served.

Buffet Service

Buffet service involves the arrangement of food on platters displayed on large tables (see Fig. 2.4). Usually a separate table is used for

Fig. 2.4. The Grand Buffet Table, Windows on the World. (*Courtesy* of Inhilco and Ezra Stoller.)

each course. Plates and silverware are conveniently arranged, and the guests serve themselves or are assisted by servers.

Buffets may be of many types. Weekend brunch buffets are very popular in some areas. A commercial restaurant may offer a special buffet lunch or dinner to boost sales on low volume days, or it may operate a buffet on a regular basis. One very popular type of service offers appetizers, salad, and breads buffet style, with the rest of the meal served at the table. Occasionally, a luxury restaurant may display menu items—usually appetizers and hors d'oeuvres—on a buffet table. The guest makes his choice, and the items selected are then plated by the waiter and served to the guest at his table. This style of service applies the merchandising aspects of the buffet to fine table service. The elegant display invites the guest to select the items shown, but he is not expected to serve himself; full service is provided. The display is also maintained throughout the meal, since the food is being plated by professional waiters rather than unpracticed guests.

Buffet service is versatile and lends itself to every type of meal from breakfast to steak roasts. It is very popular for function and group business and may be used for receptions and cocktail hours before a regular table service banquet. Teas are also a form of buffet service.

Other Types of Service

Several other types of table service are occasionally found in public restaurants and in some institutional food services. Among them are family style service and tray service.

Family Style Service

Family style service is the presentation of food in bowls or platters that are passed from hand to hand by the guests, who help themselves as they pass. This type of service is unusual in an urban restaurant but is suited to a country style operation that offers a limited menu but unlimited portions for a set price. It is in keeping with an informal, rustic theme. Family service is occasionally found in institutions. In such cases, the residents usually have no choice of entrées.

Tray Service

Tray service was once thought suitable only for feeding the sick. However, with the increasingly sophisticated food services offered on airplanes, it has lost its sickbed connotation and is often referred to as *airline service*. It is usually used in a fast service operation with a very limited menu. The server takes the order, goes to a serving pantry, and gathers everything required for the order onto a tray, making only one trip back to the guest. Clearing the table is also fast, requiring only the removal of the tray.

Combination Styles of Service

Very often, a mixture of several styles is used. Some entrées may be plated in the kitchen, while others are served as in French or Russian service. A casserole or potpie may be dished onto the plate before the guest in Russian style; a steak may be plated in the kitchen, and a flaming dish prepared on the guéridon. The guest may serve himself the first course from an hors d'oeuvre buffet table, with the rest of the meal served to him.

What is important here is not that the service is of several styles, but that the management must plan the details of service to suit the menu, the physical facilities, the kind of clientele, and the seat turnover desired. The staff must then be trained to follow these details.

Classification of Service by Means of Delivery

Service is sometimes classified by the means used to deliver the food to the guest—tray service, arm service, or cart service. In a classic French service, the food may be delivered to the guéridon by cart. This eliminates the carrying of heavy silver service pieces and also provides a place to set the loaded tray. It is also more elegant in appearance. After the finishing step, the plated food is delivered to the guest individually by hand.

Tray service may be of several types. Large trays, called *hotel ovals,* may be used in French or American service to transport food to a side stand. Because of the size of these trays, they are usually heavily loaded and carried over the shoulder. A large tray may be both an advantage and a disadvantage. A number of plates may be carried in one trip, but a waiter who is not particularly service-oriented may be tempted to delay his service until he has a full tray and thus cut down on the number of trips to the kitchen.

Small trays—either round, oval, or rectangular—are carried on one arm at waist level and are used for cocktail service and occasionally for American service of food. If properly used, these small trays are never set down. Plates are carried from the kitchen and placed directly on the table from the tray held by the server. This type of tray service is suited to low- and medium-priced operations with a more rapid turnover.

Arm service is usually found in less elegant surroundings, such as diners and coffee shops. Plated food is carried by hand directly to the table. Some servers may be inclined to stack numerous plates of food on their arms to reduce the number of trips. If plate covers are not used, this practice can result in mashed, unappetizing, and unsanitary food.

Chapter 3

Dining Room Organization

Traditional Dining Room Staffing

In the European system of staffing, the maître d'hôtel is in charge of the dining rooms and all food and beverage functions, with the exception of those supervised by the chef de cuisine. In a large restaurant or hotel, there may be one or more assistant maîtres d'hôtel who supervise different dining rooms or banquet rooms. Other subordinate management positions include

- Chef de service
- Director of service
- Chef d'etage
- Director of service on a floor
- Maître d'hôtel de carre
- Supervisor of a section of a dining room

In the dining room, the *chef de rang* (chief of the station or row of tables) is an experienced waiter who takes guests' orders and does the difficult carving and finishing of the dishes. He is responsible for the service in his station. The chef de rang has one or more assistants called *commis de rang*. The commis is a less experienced waiter who brings the food from the kitchen and assists the chef de rang by passing plated food to the guests and clearing the dirty dishes from the table. Before becoming a commis, he served as an apprentice for three years to learn the trade.

The *sommelier,* or wine steward, is in complete charge of the wine cellar. He selects the wines to be stocked by the restaurant and, during service, assists guests in making their wine selections. Actual service of the wine may be performed by the sommelier or by a captain. Occasionally the sommelier supervises a staff of assistants who may serve liquor as well as wines.

11

In the traditional hierarchy of the French dining room, each position is a training ground for the next higher level. This procedure assures a supply of labor that is well trained in all aspects of good service. It also develops a high level of professionalism in restaurant service and a pride in the profession among restaurant personnel.

Staffing in American Restaurants

Very few restaurants in the United States are staffed according to the traditional system. There are no apprenticeships or formalized routes for career advancement as there are in the European system. Those in lower level positions tend to remain in them, resulting in a stratified hierarchy and a general lack of professionalism. The standard job classifications are

- Maître d'hôtel
- Captain
- Waiter
- Busboy

The maître d'hôtel is responsible for all service in his dining room, although he may delegate direct supervision of service to his captains. He also maintains the reservation book and greets arriving guests at the door. He knows regular guests by name and is ready to provide personal service, knowing in advance their preferences.

In American restaurants offering French service, captains, waiters, and busboys usually work in teams with one captain and one busboy for every two or four waiters. The captain takes the orders and supervises the service in his station. He also performs the carving and finishing of the dishes. The waiters work in pairs, with one serving as runner to the kitchen and the other remaining at the station to attend to the guests. The busboy clears and resets the tables, pours the water, and keeps the station supplied with linen and ware.

For American or plate service, many of the captain's skills are not required, and this position is usually eliminated in a small restaurant or coffee shop.

In a large formal dining room using American service, however, captains are used to supervise the service and the seating in their assigned sections. In such situations, a maître d' is stationed at the door, and ushers are used to direct guests to the various sections of the room where they are met by the captain. At the table, the captain makes sure the menus are presented, all table appointments are in order, and cocktail orders are taken. Though a waiter may take the order, the captain is responsible for all service in his section. He may also serve wines if a sommelier is not employed. The captain may also be responsible for preparing and presenting the check.

The sommelier position usually exists in an American restaurant that offers French service. If the establishment does not have an extensive wine cellar or a sophisticated clientele, the position may be retained, but then the job is more likely a matter of fetching and serving with the wine buying done by the manager.

In dining rooms offering fast service, such as a coffee shop, the position of host or hostess is usually found. The duties of the host are not much different from those of the maître d'. The type of service, however, is much less elaborate, and there is less likely to be extensive beverage service. Also, this type of restaurant usually does not accept reservations. In a small restaurant, the host may also be responsible for cashiering.

In a large fast service restaurant, ushering and seating require the host's full attention during busy periods. In such cases, the duties of this position do not include supervision of service. The host remains at the door, and someone else—a service supervisor, room manager, or assistant manager—assumes the responsibility for the supervision of service. This person is free to move about the dining room to oversee service and is not occupied with seating guests. In such situations, the service supervisor is a management position with full line authority and responsibility for the operation of the room; the host or hostess at the door is a subordinate position, usually without authority over the staff.

Job Descriptions

Following are general job descriptions for dining room supervisory personnel:

Supervisor of Service, Director of Service, or Dining Room Manager

Reports to: General manager or owner

General Description of Duties: Supervises the operation of all dining rooms including hiring, training, and scheduling of service personnel. Maintains service standards and oversees the upkeep of physical facilities. Conducts daily lineups of service personnel. Supervises service during serving periods. Handles guest complaints. In conjunction with manager and chef, helps plan menus, controls costs (primarily payroll costs), and works to build sales. Carries out management policies within the department.

Personnel Supervised: Seating host, ushers, captains, waiters, and busboys. May also supervise banquet maître d', coat check and rest room attendants, and wine steward.

Works with: Executive chef, controller or chief cashier, executive steward or back of the house manager, and catering sales manager.

Special Skills and Qualifications: Thorough knowledge of table service techniques (including French service), food, cookery, wines, and liquors. Ability to direct personnel and administer the department. Ability to plan, including forecasting and participation in making budgets. Able to meet the public and handle complaints and problems.

Comments: Position usually found only in large operations.

Seating Host or Maître d'

Reports to: Director of service

General Description of Duties: Supervises the handling of reservations and seating of guests in a large restaurant. May supervise greeters, ushers, or telephone receptionist. Books parties in the restaurant and makes special arrangements as required.

Special Skills: Ability to deal with the public in a gracious manner; remember names, faces, and guests' preferences; have a knowledge of fine food and wines; present a good appearance; and have a pleasant speaking voice. May be required to speak more than one language, depending on clientele.

Maître d'

Reports to: General manager or owner

General Description of Duties: Supervises the overall operation of a formal dining room including hiring and training of personnel, maintaining service standards, and overseeing the upkeep of physical facilities. Receives reservations, keeps reservation book, greets guests at the door, and supervises seating. May also plan and book private parties. Helps with menu planning, cost control, and works to build sales volume.

Personnel Supervised: Captains, waiters, and busboys. May also supervise the wine steward.

Works with: Chef, chief steward, chief cashier, or controller. May also work with banquet manager if there is a large banquet business.

Special Skills and Qualifications: Thorough knowledge of table service techniques (including French service), food, cookery, wines, and liquors. Ability to direct personnel and administer the department. Ability to deal with the public in a gracious manner; remember names, faces, and guests' preferences; present a good appearance; and have a pleasant speaking voice. May be required to speak more than one language, depending on clientele.

Comments: More often found in smaller, formal restaurants.

Host or Hostess

Reports to: General manager or owner (May report to a director of service in a multirestaurant complex.)

General Description of Duties: Supervises the operation of a coffee shop or informal table service restaurant. Maintains standards of service and oversees the upkeep of physical facilities. Hires, trains, and schedules staff. Conducts daily lineups of staff, supervises service during meal periods, and handles guest complaints. Oversees the door, seats guests, and controls waiting lines. May also supervise cashiers or act as cashier.

Supervises: Waiters, waitresses, and busboys. May also supervise assistant host or seating host in a large operation.

Special Skills and Qualifications: Ability to meet the public in a gracious manner, supervise the staff, and administer the department. Should be able to handle complaints and problems. Should present a good appearance—neat and well groomed. Some knowledge of food and cookery is usually required, as well as knowledge of table service techniques. Knowledge of alcoholic beverage service may also be required.

Chapter 4

Standards of Service

In a well-run dining room, the standards of service are clearly defined. These standards include the following:

1. The steps of service: procedures for taking orders, delivering food, and clearing tables
2. The details of the service, that is, the proper table setting and the ware and accompaniments to be used in the service of each menu item
3. Merchandising and selling procedures (discussed in Chap. 6)
4. Staff behavior and appearance

Steps of Service

The following are the basic steps necessary in serving a guest:

1. Seating and presenting the menu
2. Cocktail service, if available
3. Taking the orders
4. Placing on the table the water, rolls, relishes, or other items required by the style of service
5. Placing the orders with the kitchen and obtaining them
6. Preparing and presenting the check and collecting the money
7. Clearing the table and resetting for the next customer

Seating and Presenting the Menu

Seating the guests is usually done by a maître d' or host, who also presents the menu (if there is one). If guests seat themselves, the waiter must present the menu. In some fast service restaurants, the menu is posted on the wall or on a placemat. Some pub-like restaurants also use a chalkboard or wallboard. The waiter usually draws the guests' attention to it, pointing out the specials or reciting them if they are not listed.

16

Cocktail Service

When cocktail service is offered, either the host or the server may ask if a cocktail is desired. After the order is taken, the server goes to the bar, places the order, and obtains and serves the drink. Very often the glassware for the drinks is stored outside of the bartender's reach, and the server must give him the proper glassware. This is done when space behind the bar is limited. It also eliminates the need for bar porters and busboys, who are replenishing the supply of clean glassware, to enter the bartender's work area. The serving person must know which glass to use for each kind of drink and should also recognize the finished drinks by sight. In some high-volume bars, the servers also garnish the drinks— adding the olives, fruit, swizzlers, and so forth as required. An identification system should be devised so that the bartender and the servers can identify drinks made with "call" brands. Some bartenders use colored swizzle sticks to identify them. Failure to serve the brand ordered can cause guest dissatisfaction, particularly when a premium-priced liquor is involved.

When serving drinks, the waiter should not have to ask the guests what they ordered. One system for keeping track of orders is to establish one point in the room, such as the door, as a starting base. All seats facing that point are designated as number one, with the other seats numbered consecutively clockwise around the table. If the guests at seats number two and number four are ladies, their orders can be taken first but are designated according to their seat numbers. This way the right drink can be served to each guest without interrupting the conversation to ask, "Who gets the Bloody Mary?"

After the cocktail order has been served, the waiter should stay alert for some signal from the guest that another round of drinks is desired or that he is ready to order the meal. In some operations, the waiter approaches the guest for a reorder when glasses are three-quarters empty. In a cocktail lounge especially, an alert staff can increase sales (and tips) with prompt refills.

Taking the Orders

In fast service restaurants, the menu is often posted outside or at the door, and the guest may be ready to give his order as soon as he is seated. Usually, however, the guests like to look over the menu and make their selection at their leisure. While they are doing this, the waiter or busboy can fill the water glasses and serve the butter, breads or crackers, relishes, or any other items required by the style of service. When the guest turns his attention from the menu, he is ready to give his order.

Orders may be written directly on a guest check, on a special preprinted form, or on a captain's order pad. Orders are usually taken from the ladies first, although some women may prefer to have their escorts order for them. The system described for taking drink orders can also be used for taking food orders. If the whole staff uses the same system, any waiter can serve an order taken by another. This is especially important when waiters work in teams.

To speed order taking and minimize errors, a common set of abbreviations should be established. One code, known to and used by all, is essential to the quick and accurate preparation of orders by the cooks. A standard code also makes the auditing of checks easier and more accurate.

Sometimes items are numbered on the menu for fast ordering. If numbers and abbreviations are used on the guest check, they should give sufficient indication of what the item is, so the guest can tell what he is being charged for.

A sample list of abbreviations for a coffee shop menu follows. Items are listed in the order in which they appear on the menu.

Breakfast Menu

Fruit slices	$.75
O.j, G.j, T.j	.35
V.j	.55
Apple	.60
Grapefruit	.60
Cereal	.55
Cereal fruit	.85
#1	
(j + bri or dan + coffee or tea)	
#2	1.50
(j + skill + coffee or tea)	
Eggs might be: scram	
over 1	
over e	
over m	
over w	
sunny	
poach	
#3	1.75
(j or grapefruit + sau & biscuit + coffee or tea)	
#4	2.25
(j + blintzes + coffee or tea)	
Bac roll	.95
Egg sand	.75
Bri	.50
Dan	.50

Muf corn		.35
Muf bran		.35
Muf fruit		.40
Eng muf		.35
Roll		.35
Bag/butter		.35
Bag/cr cheese		.35
Bag/tst		.35
Bag		.35
Scram 2		.95
Fry 2		
over 1		.95
over e		
over m		
over w		
sunny		
Scram 3 or Fry 3		1.15
Ome/bac ch		1.55
Ome/farm		1.55
Pancake		.90
Pancake	Fry 1	1.10
Pancake stack/sau		1.20
Fr/tst		.95
Fr/tst bac		1.55
Fr/tst ham		1.55
Fr/tst sau		1.55
Sau	(add)	.60
Bac	(add)	.60
Ham	(add)	.60
Coffee		.30
Tea		.30
Sanka		.30
Choco		.35
Milk		.35
Soft drinks		.40
Iced tea		.45
Iced coffee		.45
Es		.50
Cappu		.65

Placing the Orders with the Kitchen and Obtaining Them

Orders must be transmitted clearly to the kitchen to avoid errors or misunderstandings. If some items must be prepared to order, the waiters should know how long these orders take and coordinate them so that the party's order will all be ready at the same time. In many of the busier kitchens, the chef or his assistant does this coordinating or expediting at the range. (In the French kitchen, this position is known as the *abboyeur* or barker.) The expediter receives the written orders from the waiters and gives them to the proper stations, such as the broiler cook, roast cook, fry cook, or vegetable cook. The expediter also coordinates the timing of the various orders, approves the dishes going out, and provides some control by seeing that no food is dispensed without being recorded on a guest check.

After the waiter has put in his orders at the range, he assembles his first course orders on his tray, drawing the hot soups last so that they are still hot when served. If no appetizers or soups are ordered, the salad is sometimes served in its place, especially if the entree is prepared to order.

The waiter may dish up and garnish some items himself. Spoons, tongs, and forks should always be used to handle food. The service procedure should specify the portion sizes for items dished up by waiters. Some waiters mistake generous portions for good service and think that serving extra-large helpings of rolls, butter, cream, jelly, and so forth will increase their tips. The dining room supervisor should be alert to waste of this nature. Management should establish a policy on the service of extra-large helpings, how much is to be served when requested and what, if anything, is to be charged for such requests.

When picking up orders in the kitchen, all cold items should be picked first and hot foods, last. The tray should be loaded so that the weight is balanced. Whenever possible, the items should be arranged in order of the service. For American service, the entrees should be covered and stacked in the same order in which they will be served. This procedure will provide quick, efficient service with a minimum of delay, thus preventing hot food from getting cold. All accompanying items should be collected and taken on the same trip. It helps if things that are served together are kept together. This saves steps and time. The waiter doesn't have to return to the kitchen for a forgotten fork or sauce, while the guest sits looking at his food.

The organization of one's tray and one's station should be stressed when training new waiters. Before leaving his station to go to the kitchen, the waiter should check the progress of each party and anticipate its needs. If one group is almost finished with the appetizers, they may be ready for the main course before the waiter returns from the kitchen. If the orders are ready, they can be brought immediately. This is what is meant by organization of the station. As the cliché goes, "Use your head and save your feet."

Preparing and Presenting the Check and Collecting the Money

In many operations, the check must be made out and properly priced before the waiter can pick up his orders from the range. This is known as prechecking. There are various other methods of controlling guest checks and cash. Since this is an important aspect of internal control, it is discussed separately in Chap. 13.

Clearing the Table and Resetting for the Next Customer

The faster the table is cleared and reset after the guest has left, the sooner the next party can be seated. In some establishments, clearing is left solely to the bus help. A smart waiter knows that the faster his tables are reset, the more guests he can serve and the more tips he will make. Where union regulations permit, waiters should be encouraged to bus their own tables whenever they can. Taking dirty dishes when going to the kitchen does not take any more time than going with an empty tray. Furthermore, uncleared tables are unsightly and detract from the appearance of the dining room.

In some types of operations, guests may be seated at uncleared tables. This should only be done when it cannot be avoided—as in fast turnover, high-volume operations such as coffee shops.

The proper way to clear or bus a table should be established. If silverware is separated and plates scraped and stacked as the table is cleared, dishwashing becomes much more efficient, and breakage costs are reduced. Noise levels in the dining room are also lowered.

When the tablecloth is changed during service, it should be done discreetly, without a flourish that could be distracting to nearby guests. The correct way to change a tablecloth is to fold back one edge of the soiled cloth and position the clean cloth on the uncovered edge of the table. The soiled cloth is then folded as the clean cloth is unfolded in position on the table. Crumbs are wrapped in the soiled cloth rather than shaken onto the floor or seats (see Fig. 4.1).

Tablecloths are always changed without exposing the unclothed table top and without placing anything on the chairs. Proceed as follows:

1. As soon as guests have left, set tray on side stand next to table. The fresh tablecloth should be tucked under your arm to avoid making a second trip.
2. Remove everything from the table. Place all glassware, dishware, silverware, and linen on the bus tray. (Be sure to remove glasses without handling the rims or insides.)
3. Pull table out if it is against a wall.

4. Take into your hands the fresh, folded tablecloth (which should have been under your arm as you did the above).
5. Partially unfold the fresh cloth; hold it at the ends.
6. Reach over the table and grasp the ends of the soiled cloth (sides opposite you).

Fig. 4.1. How to change a tablecloth: a task description from the training manual of The Market Dining Room. (*Courtesy* of The Market Bar and Dining Rooms and Inhilco.)

7. In one motion, slide the soiled cloth off and lay the fresh cloth without exposing the table surface.
8. Roll up soiled cloth into a tight, neat roll.
9. Put soiled cloth under your arm.
10. Straighten out fresh cloth so it is hanging evenly on all sides.
11. Move table back in place.
12. Wipe salt and pepper and place on clean cloth with clean ash tray.
13. Remove crumbs from the seats (using the rolled cloth) into your hands, never on the floor.
14. Put rolled cloth on tray and remove tray and side stand.
15. Bring settings to table—dishware, silverware, and napkins in one hand; glass stems in the other hand. Learn to carry everything in one trip.
16. Set table.

Note: *Never* bring fresh settings to the table before you have changed the tablecloth because you will have no place to set them down. *Nothing should be placed on chairs.*

Table Settings

For many years etiquette has dictated the correct way of setting a table. Although standards of etiquette may change over time, people have come to look for certain table implements in certain places. Minor variations can be devised to suit the merchandising plan of a certain restaurant, but they should not be too different from the accepted pattern. Figures 4.2, 4.3, and 4.4 illustrate three styles of table setting: formal, informal, and banquet.

If tablecloths are used, a silence pad is put on the table first. This is a cloth of felt or other thick material that cushions the surface and muffles the sound of china and silver on the table top. Some table tops are covered with a cushioned plastic that serves the same purpose. In many restaurants an undercloth is also used to hide the less presentable silence pad when the cloth is changed during the meal period. In addition, by using a larger undercloth, the top cloth can be smaller, saving on laundry costs.

The dining room supervisor is responsible for seeing that there is an adequate supply of table linen of the proper sizes. He may deal directly with the laundry in placing orders, or he may give his order to a steward, housekeeper, or manager.

Paper placemats and napkins may be used in place of linen. Some fast service operations even eliminate the placemats and put all the silverware on the napkin. Putting silverware directly on the bare table is not an acceptable sanitary practice.

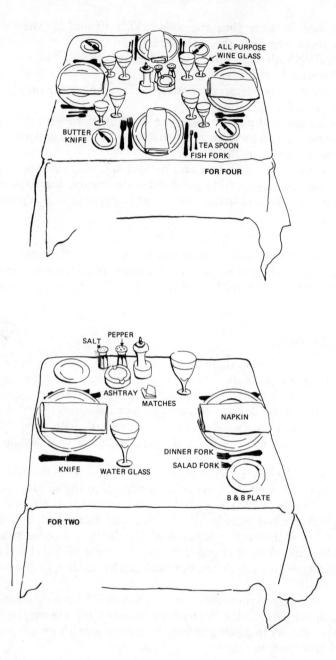

Fig. 4.2. Formal table setting. (*Courtesy* of The Market Dining Room, The Corner, and Inhilco.)

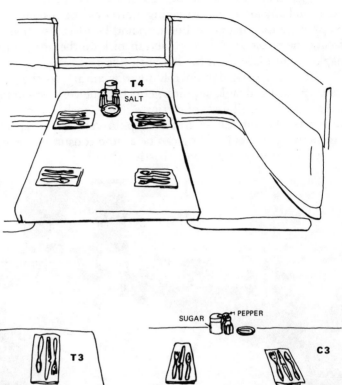

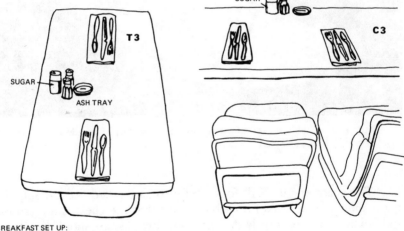

BREAKFAST SET UP:
  CUP AND SAUCER TO RIGHT OF PAPER NAPKINS
LUNCH SET UP:
  LINEN NAPKINS

Fig. 4.3.   Informal table setting. (*Courtesy* of The Market Dining Room, The Corner, and Inhilco.)

Placemats are usually set about two inches from the edge of the table, and any art work or reading matter on them should face the guest. Napkins, either paper or linen, should be placed so that one corner is facing the guest. In this way, he can pick up the open corner, open the napkin, and place it on his lap with one hand.

In years past, napkin folding was an art. In the late nineteenth century, food and table appointments became very ostentatious. Napkins were folded into all sorts of intricate shapes such as fans, flowers, swans, and hats. An intricately folded napkin can add to an attractive and distinctive table, but folding can be a time-consuming operation and, at today's labor wage rates, very costly.

Fig. 4.4.   A table set for a formal banquet. (*Courtesy* of Windows on the World, Inhilco, and Ezra Stoller.)

The space and utensils for each person are called a *cover*. Sufficient space should be allowed for each cover so that the guest is not crowded and can be served promptly. At least 24 inches of space should be allowed. The arrangement of the items required for the cover should be balanced and attractive.

Silverware is arranged about two inches from the edge of the table. The accepted placement of the knives, forks, and spoons is based on the European style of eating in which utensils used with the left hand (fork) are placed on the left and those used with the right hand (knife and spoon) are placed on the right. Americans eat in a less efficient manner, with the fork held in the left hand for cutting food and switched to the right hand for transporting the food to the mouth. However, the placement of silverware on the table remains in the European style. The pieces are arranged in the order of use, starting from the outside.

The pieces of china and silver used should depend on the requirements of the meal. At a banquet, only the pieces actually required by the menu are set, however, in dining rooms, a standard setting must be established. (A knife is always set, whether the menu warrants it or not, since it is required by the European style of eating.) Different standard settings may be used for different meals.

A center setup consists of sugar bowl, ash tray, matches, salt and pepper shakers, and sometimes a bud vase or condiment bottles. It may also contain a napkin dispenser, though these are more often found in self-service or fast food operations. Sugar bowls and salt and pepper shakers are placed in the center of a table that seats four and along one side of tables for two. If the table for two is a wall table, the side toward the wall is the one to use. If it is not a wall table, the side away from the main traffic aisle should be used for this purpose.

Ash trays stocked with matches belong alongside the sugar bowls. When the table is cleared, the ash trays should be cleaned and restocked with matches whenever necessary. If the ash trays are used, they must be replaced with clean trays as often as necessary during the meal.

Details of Service

The details of service should be spelled out for each item on the menu. If there are special orders (nonlisted items) that are frequently served, instructions should be included for these items as well.

These details of service should be compiled and given to each trainee and also posted at the appropriate point in the kitchen and pantry. Dining room supervisors should review the details of service at lineups from time to time and should be alert to an incorrect service during meal periods. Improper service should be corrected in the kitchen, obviously, and not in the presence of the guests.

Following are several examples of service details:

Soup—Cup

Serve one ladle of soup, dipped from the bottom of the pot, into a soup cup. Follow the instructions given in lineup for garnishing. Serve on a saucer for an underliner. Serve a bouillon spoon. Be sure there are crackers in the roll basket, and offer another basket if there are none.

Soup—Plate

Serve one and one-half ladles, dipped from the bottom of the pot. Use an eight-inch underliner and serve with a soup spoon. Follow other directions for a cup of soup.

Shrimp Cocktail

Fill supreme dish with crushed ice, cover with ring, and place insert dish in the ring. Be sure the cocktail has five shrimp. Use a seven-inch underliner with paper doily. Serve one lemon wedge on the underliner. Be sure there are crackers in the roll basket. Offer another basket if there are none.

Salad, Tossed Green

Served in a wooden bowl. Place salad dressing rack on the table when salads are served.

Entrées

Eight-inch plates are used at lunch; nine-inch, at dinner. Garnishes will be specified at lineup for the various daily entrées. Standard items are listed below.

Lamb chops. Mint sauce in a relish boat and steak knife. Mint jelly available on request.

Steaks. Steak knife. Steak sauce available on request.

Chopped steak. Catsup in a relish boat on request.

All hot plates are to be covered when taken to the dining room.

Pies

Served on seven-inch liner. Set the pie so the point faces the guest. Serve a place fork.

Ice Cream

Served in an ice cream dish. Use a seven-inch underliner with paper doily. One cookie on the underliner. Serve a place spoon.

Coffee

Serve individual pots of coffee for each order. Offer to pour the first cup. Serve a small pitcher of cream for one or two guests and a large pitcher for three or four.

Service Staff Behavior and Appearance

While a long list of "thou shalt nots" can be a source of poor morale, certain standards of behavior are essential to good service. Smoking, eating, drinking, and gum chewing while on duty should not be allowed. When they are not busy with service, waiters should be at their stations and alert to the needs of their guests. They should not be permitted to congregate in the kitchen or in a corner of the dining room where loud conversation can be distracting to nearby guests.

Food is not appetizing if served by a person who is slovenly or unclean. Uniforms must be clean and well-pressed. Lightweight uniforms should be changed daily. If food is spilled on uniforms, some provision should be made for quick changes. Hands and fingernails should always be clean and well-groomed. Hair should be clean and neatly styled. Long, loose hair arrangements have no place in a food service operation. Many departments of health require caps or hairnets for food service workers. Daily baths are necessary, and the use of a deodorant for both waiters and waitresses cannot be stressed too firmly. Good dental care is also important. Breath sweetener or mouthwash should be used before going on duty.

Needless to say, work rules should not be made for their own sake but rather for the purpose of providing good service to the guest. They should be uniformly and fairly enforced by the dining room supervisor.

Breakdown of Service

When standards of service are not met, we say that a *breakdown* in service has occurred. There are a number of causes of breakdowns, many of which are not the fault of the waiter.

Poor Seating

When a waiter's station is all seated at once, he may get "stuck" through no fault of his own. If seating is staggered, he can devote attention to each table in turn. There are times, however, when it is impossible to avoid seating a full station, or even a whole dining room, in a very short period. Most guests are willing to wait if their presence is acknowledged by the server. He may say, "Good evening, I'll be with you in just a moment." No one likes to be ignored. The supervisor should be alert to potential breakdowns caused by the seating pattern and should get help for the waiter.

Physical Layout

Bottlenecks in the kitchen may be a cause of service breakdowns. If the kitchen is a long way from the dining room, team service may be required. In this way, at least one waiter is on the station at all times to attend to the guests.

Sometimes only minor changes in the kitchen layout will eliminate a serious bottleneck. If this is not possible, it may be desirable to move some activities that create the bottleneck. For example, you might use carts to drop off dirty dishes instead of carrying them to a congested dish washing area or move the coffee-making function to the dining room with single-pot brewing equipment instead of one large coffee station.

Shortage of Ware

Some managers feel they save money by operating with a shortage of silver, china, and glassware. This is a bad practice. It can cause poor staff morale and poor service to the guest. Waiters may resort to carrying silverware and other equipment in their pockets—an unsanitary and unprofessional practice. They may also take it from each other's station, bribe busboys and warewashers, or resort to washing their own ware. This last practice is the least desired of all. It takes the waiter's time when he should be attending to his guest. In addition, he cannot achieve the level of sanitation of machine washing.

Poor Communication with the Kitchen

When orders are given verbally to the kitchen, there is always a chance for error. Items can be misordered, misunderstood, not heard at all, or completely forgotten. When cooks take orders directly from the waiters, there could be a deliberate foul-up if there is a personality conflict. Some operations have found the use of mechanical communication devices, such as the tel-autograph or pneumatic tubes, very helpful in transporting written orders to a distant kitchen. Some of the new electronic cash register systems have remote printing devices which can print the order in the kitchen as the waiter enters it on the register.

Waits or Runouts

Delays in preparation or runouts of food are beyond the control of the dining room supervisor. He can only insist that the kitchen communicate this information to the waiters as quickly as possible and that the waiters report to the guests for a possible change of orders. Most kitchens use a blackboard for posting the status of items during the meal period. Frequent problems of runouts or delays should be referred to management for correction.

Accidents

Accidents are inevitable, but they can be kept to a minimum by a staff that is trained to be safety conscious. Spills should be wiped up immediately and floors kept clean. Nonskid surfaces can be installed on floors that are particularly hazardous, such as in dishrooms or on ramps.

Personnel should be trained to announce their presence when passing others loaded with trays and should use such phrases as "passing please," "behind you," or "hot coffee."

When an accident has occurred that will delay service, the supervisor should inform the guest and offer apologies to avoid dissatisfaction. Most guests will be understanding if they know the reason for the delay.

Chapter 5

Dining Room Operation

Thus far we have discussed the technical aspects of service. This chapter deals with the technical side of running a dining room and includes information on maintaining the premises, assigning stations, holding lineups to brief the staff, seating guests, assigning sidework, record keeping (scheduling the staff and preparing payroll information), and controlling costs.

Dining Room Inspection

The appearance and condition of the dining room should be checked before each meal. The dining room supervisor should allow enough time to make this inspection and correct any unacceptable conditions before the dining room opens. Problems with air conditioning, heating, or ventilation should be referred to the manager or maintenance department for immediate action. Some last minute cleaning or replenishing of supplies and wares may be required. The supervisor should also be alert to potential safety hazards and correct them immediately.

Some companies use a check list for this purpose. This helps anyone substituting in the job. The check list provides a written plan for that specific dining room. Check lists will vary depending on the type of operation, equipment, and architectural details in the room. The major items to be checked in most food service operations are as follows:

- Doors
- Cashier's station
- Floors and carpets
- Walls
- Table settings
- Ash trays, sugar bowls, salts, and peppers

- Menus
- Lamps and lamp shades
- Windows
- Curtains, shades, and draperies
- Mirrors and pictures
- Table linen
- Chairs (including reserve high chairs)
- Condiment containers
- Table legs (for steadiness)
- Table cloths (for even hanging)
- Table legs and chair legs (for splinters)
- Side stands and supplies

The room's light, heat, and ventilation should also be checked.

Don't limit your inspection to the inside of the building. Many restaurants have dining rooms or lobbies that are visible from the street. The view presented to pedestrians can be a strong selling tool or a total turnoff. Dead bugs and dust on the window sill tell potential guests something about the cleanliness of the kitchen. A view of an attractively setup dining room may entice the passerby to come back for dinner, but messy looking tables with last night's soiled tablecloths will not appeal.

Assigning Stations

The seats and tables assigned to each waiter or team of waiters are called a *station*. The number of tables assigned will depend on the number of seats, the frequency of their turnover, the competence of the particular waiter, the distance to the kitchen, and the number of waiters scheduled for the particular meal. At a fast turnover counter operation, a waiter may only be able to handle six or seven seats even though the distance to the pickup areas may be only a few feet. On the other hand, in a dining room with only a moderate turnover and an even flow of patrons, a waiter may be able to serve as many as 16 to 20 seats (see Figs. 5.1 and 5.2).

In some dining rooms, stations are fixed and permanently assigned to each waiter. A relief waiter, usually one with little seniority, relieves each station on that waiter's day off. The fixed station system is usually unfair to younger members of the staff because they are limited to the less desirable stations. Once this system is in practice, however, it is very difficult to change.

A more flexible and equitable arrangement is to rotate stations and vary the station size according to the volume of business expected and the number of waiters scheduled. Every dining room has some seats and stations that are more desirable to the guests than others, and it is quite impractical to try to force the guests onto the less desirable stations when more attractive seats are available. Although stations can be planned to balance some of the work load, the rotation of stations among the staff is a more equitable way of balancing the work.

When a lower volume of business is forecast and the dining room is not staffed to capacity, station assignment can be enlarged. In this way, the entire room is assigned even though the number of waiters is reduced.

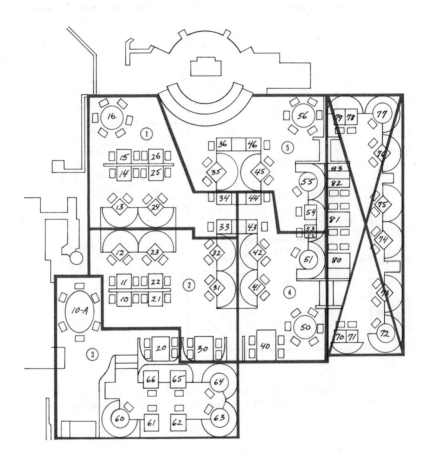

Fig. 5.1. This and Fig. 5.2. are station charts for The Market Dining Room in the World Trade Center, New York. This shows the stations when five waiters are scheduled. (*Courtesy* of The Market Bar and Dining Rooms and Inhilco.)

Sections of the room can be closed off, depending on the architectural plan of the room and the expected flow of business. A smaller room that is kept full provides a better image and atmosphere than a large room that is a sea of tablecloths in slower periods (see Figs. 5.1 and 5.2).

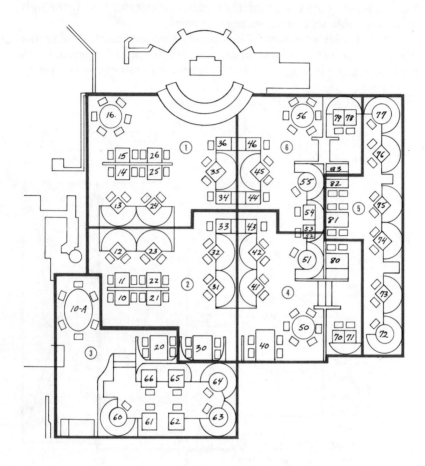

Fig. 5.2. This shows the stations from Fig. 5.1. when six teams of waiters are used. (*Courtesy* of The Market Bar and Dining Rooms and Inhilco.)

Lineups

Lineups are short dining room staff meetings at which the staff is inspected for neatness of dress and personal cleanliness (see Fig. 5.3). Station assignments are usually made at that time, and the service staff is briefed on the menu for the day. This briefing should include the following:

1. The prices of all menu items, their contents, and the method of preparation
2. A discussion of made-to-order items

3. The location in the kitchen where an item is to be found
4. The approximate time required to wait for items prepared to order
5. The items that should be promoted and any planned substitutes in the event of runouts
6. The tasting of new dishes and instruction for their service
7. A review of the correct service of other menu items
8. A discussion of any guest complaints pertaining to service

Fig. 5.3. Captains, waiters, waitresses, and busboys of Windows on the World at daily lineup. (*Courtesy* of Windows on the World and Inhilco.)

Seating

When seating guests, the host must consider any special needs or requests of the guest, the status of service on each station at that moment, and the number of guests each station already has.

When seating a guest with a special need, that need must always come first. For instance, a guest who is disabled or feeble should be seated close to the door so he will not have to navigate through a dining room full of furniture. A family with small children needs a quiet table off to the side where the youngsters won't bother other guests. A television personality or local politician may want to sit at center stage where he can see and be seen, or he may want privacy.

Most guests don't need that kind of special consideration. They just want a good table where they can get good service. Unless another table is clearly preferable to the one assigned to them, they will accept the assigned table. If arriving guests are seated in each station in rotation, each waiter can devote his attention to each of his tables in turn. Furthermore, each waiter will receive about the same number of guests and therefore have a fairly equal share of the work load and the tips. Unfortunately, it doesn't always work that smoothly, and the host should always be aware of the status of service on a station before he seats another party there. If the waiter is stuck (unable to deliver the desired level of service for any reason), giving him more people will only make him more stuck and further delay service to the guests he already has. *Seating must always be in consideration of the guest and not the staff.*

Although the host should try to give each waiter an equal chance to make his tips, in every crew there are one or more waiters who are able to handle more covers than the others. These more productive workers should not be penalized.

When guests seat themselves, a more flexible station assignment is needed to spread the work load and the tips and to give the best service to all guests. One way to accomplish this is to assign fewer seats to a station that is more popular than others. Another way is to have waiters work in teams, covering sections of the room rather than individual stations. Tips may be shared by the entire crew by pooling.

Controlling Breakage and Linen Costs

Although much of the china and glassware breakage takes place in the dishroom, it may not all be the fault of the dishroom personnel. Badly stacked trays and poor sorting of ware by waiters and busboys can be the cause of a breakage problem. Mishandling of linen can also cause stained, worn tablecloths and napkins. If linens are allowed to get wet with water or wine, the fabric can rot or be permanently stained before it is processed by the laundry.

The staff should also be trained to use care in emptying ash trays. A live ash or smoldering butt is a potential source of fires. The National Fire Protection Association ranks cigarette sparks in trash or linen hampers as a major cause of restaurant fires.

There is a right and a wrong way to stack a tray or bus box. On a tray, silverware is sorted and laid together on the side. Plates are scraped and stacked in order of size in the middle of the tray. Cups are stacked around the outside, never more than two high. Glassware is also placed around the rim of the tray. Glasses should never be stacked since they may stick together. Paper placemats and napkins are wadded up and put on top. If table linen is used, linen napkins are tucked under the arm to prevent them from getting wet (see Fig. 5.4).

Bus boxes are usually used only in fast service dining rooms; the principles of sorting and stacking are the same as when trays are used. Busboys should be trained not to dump a whole table full of ware into a bus box. It is not only hard on the ware, it is also hard on the guests' ears and nerves.

Fig. 5.4.   Loading of tray for dessert bussing. Paper placemats and napkins wadded up on top, linen tucked under arm. Heaviest weights (stacked plates, silver, and coffee pot) over the shoulder or arm. Glasses and cups around the edge.

In the dishroom the busboy or waiter is usually required to sort the glassware and put it into glass racks, put the silverware into a soak pan or sink, and put the linen into a linen hamper. Sometimes he is required to stack the plates by size on the dish table. Whether or not he does this will depend on the size of the operation and the number of dishroom personnel.

Linen cost control involves correct use of clean linen as well as preventing damage to soiled linen. The use of napkins as side towels or for cleaning should be strictly forbidden. Another source of unnecessary cost is the use of cloths that are larger than needed for the table. General carelessness in handling of clean linens is another source of loss. Commercial laundries will usually give credit for linens that are unusable because of stains, tears, or holes. The staff should be trained to put such linens aside for credit.

The dining room supervisor's responsibility for his staff's performance does not end at the kitchen door. He must train his people to handle linen and ware properly and to follow through on supervision. In this area, he will need to work with the executive steward or back-of-the-house manager.

Sidework

Sidework is the name given to the dining room housekeeping jobs usually performed by the service staff. Since time spent in this work does not produce tips directly, some waiters object to doing it. Unfortunately, they do not realize that poor housekeeping affects the appearance of the room, the efficiency of service, and future sales. Typical sidework jobs include cleaning the salts, peppers, and sugar bowls; care of condiments and containers; polishing silver; dusting, straightening, and replenishing side stands; care of flowers or plants; polishing table tops; and care of decorative items in the room (see Fig. 5.5).

These jobs may be scheduled daily or weekly and should be specifically assigned on a rotating basis. Posting a weekly schedule of sidework assignments usually eliminates any misunderstandings. Written instructions for each task should be posted so everyone understands what is involved in each job (see Fig. 5.6).

A sample description of station closing duties for a coffee shop operation follows (used by permission of Inhilco):

Replenish Salt, Pepper, Sugar, and Condiments

Carry shakers, sugar bowls, and condiments on a cocktail tray to the far corner and do the work there. Do *not* do at stations in front of customers.

1. Refill salt and pepper shakers and sugar bowls to the very top. Refill over cocktail tray to avoid spills onto floor. Clean top, sides, and bottom of shakers and sugar bowls.

2. Marry catsups and mustards. Do not fill to the very top, only to the manufacturer's full level. Completely clean all condiment bottles, inside and outside of bottle necks, and inside and outside of bottle caps. Do this with a damp rag—do not get water in the bottles. If

necessary, get additional condiments from the storeroom to replenish each station with

- Four catsup (full bottles)
- Two mustard (full bottles)
- One worcestershire sauce
- One tabasco

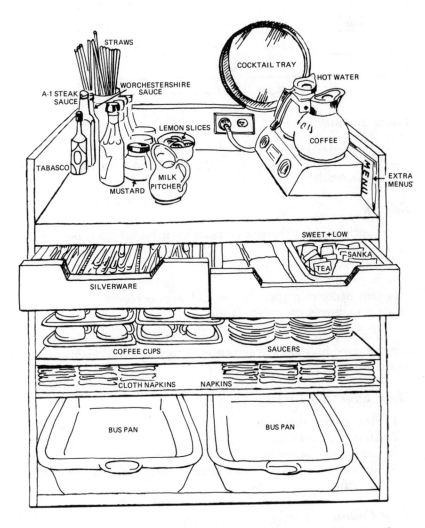

Fig. 5.5. Correct side stand setup for lunch in The Corner. (*Courtesy* of The Corner and Inhilco.)

	SUN	MON	TUES	WED	THUR	FRI	SAT
SALTS, PEPPERS, AND SUGAR BOWLS	Mary	Steve	Sheila	Sal	Maria	Willie	Charley
DUSTING WOODWORK, WINDOW SILLS, AND RAILINGS	Linda	Mary	Steve	Jose	Sheila	Paul	Willie
CONDIMENT BOTTLES	Paul	Willie	Mary	Steve	Jose	Sal	Maria
CLEAN AND RESTOCK SIDESTAND #1	Maria	Paul	Ruth	Mary	Steve	Jose	Sal
CLEAN AND RESTOCK SIDESTAND #2	CLOSED	CLOSED	Sal	Sheila	Charley	Linda	CLOSED
WASH HIGH CHAIRS AND BOOSTER SEATS	Willie	Linda	Paul	Charley	Mary	Steve	Jose
DINING ROOM REFRIGERATOR	Sheila	Ruth	Jose	Marie	Willie	Charley	Linda
FLOWERS	Ruth	Sheila	Charley	Ruth	Sal	Maria	Paul

Fig. 5.6. Sidework assignments.

Clean Station

1. Wipe all exposed shelf surfaces.
2. Clean coffee warmer—top, sides, and bottom—and shelf underneath it.

Restock

- Lunch napkins (leave two bundles of folded linen per station)
- Sanka
- Tea
- Sugar substitute
- Jam packets (grape, orange, and strawberry)
- Cocktail tray on every station

You should always leave a station in the same condition in which you found it—fully stocked and clean. If the station is closing for the day, do the following:

Clean Counters/Tables

1. Strip completely bare.
2. Clean top and edges.
3. Clean four inches into bottom of tables.
4. Remove all items from side stand counter, clean thoroughly, and set up again.

Reset Counters/Tables

1. Place clean ash tray, shakers, and sugar bowls on counter/table. Use one setup per table or per every two counter seats.
2. Set for next day. Place cups face down.

Store Perishable Items

1. Whenever possible, marry cream and milk, juices, lemon slices, and fruit salad into stations that are still open.
2. If not possible, tightly cover lemon slices with plastic wrap and put in island refrigerator.
3. Always refill juice pitchers (two orange, one grapefruit, and one tomato), tightly cover with plastic wrap, and store in island refrigerator. Discard any remaining cream and milk in pitchers. Use clean pitchers every night.
4. Give remaining cake and fruit salad to the kitchen.

Miscellaneous

1. Unplug coffee warmers. Wash pots and fill halfway with water.
2. Arrange shelves underneath the counters.

Fridays Only

1. Empty salt, pepper, and sugar into pitchers. Cover with plastic wrap and label. Put shakers and sugar bowls into bus pans for washing. Do not do this in front of customers.
2. Wash coffee pots in the dishwasher.
3. Store unopened dairy containers and whole lemons in the walk-in.
4. Discard any remaining juice in pitchers, opened dairy containers, lemon slices, and cake.

Dining Room Record Keeping

The dining room supervisor does not usually have much paperwork, but he has several important clerical tasks.

Staff Schedules and Payroll Records

Schedules should be posted well in advance so workers can make their personal plans. Accurate records of time worked must be kept. Scheduling and payroll record keeping are discussed in Chap. 10.

Cover Counts

As guests are seated, the maître d' or seating host records the number of guests assigned to each waiter or station. At the close of the meal, these counts are totaled. They provide a means of measuring each waiter's productivity. The total count is also a control tool. It is compared to the cashier's count for the meal to determine that payment was collected from each guest seated. If there is a discrepancy, the cashier can then compare the counts by waiter or station to determine who was responsible.

Dining Room Logbook

The supervisor's logbook is a very important record of daily department activity. This log should be a bound book with at least a page for each day. In it, the supervisor on each shift records all pertinent information about the day's business: the weather, cover counts, special parties, guest complaints and how they were handled, accidents, personnel matters, maintenance requests, and so forth. Where there is more than one shift of operation, the logbook becomes a primary means of communication to keep each supervisor informed about events and activities on other shifts. Over a longer period of time, the logbook can be used for planning and forecasting; for checking up on maintenance requests; and for documenting accident claims, labor union grievances, or court cases. A history of guest complaints can identify areas where greater management attention is needed or indicate a service technique or menu item that should be changed.

Other Types of Paperwork

These may include accident reports, employee disciplinary warnings, hiring requests, and employment terminations. All are discussed in later chapters.

Legal Aspects of Dining Room Operation

Government has been playing a larger role in the day-to-day operation of all businesses. Here is a sampling of the types of legislation affecting restaurants.

Federal

- OSHA—The Williams-Steiger Occupational Safety and Health Act of 1970
- EEOC regulations pertaining to equal employment opportunity legislation
- Federal minimum wage and hour legislation
- Fair employment practices laws
- The Privacy Act of 1974

State and Local

- Alcoholic beverage control regulations (liquor laws)
- Department of health sanitation regulations
- Fire department and occupancy codes
- Sunday blue laws

- Consumer protection legislation such as antismoking and truth-in-menu

In addition, a restaurant can be involved in a civil law suit because of a supervisor's or employee's action (or inaction). Civil suits usually are on the grounds of negligent conditions (causing the plaintiff illness, accident, or theft of property) or sometimes for slander or false arrest.

Safety

Federal law requires that we provide a safe working environment for our employees; common sense demands that we maintain safe premises for everyone who enters. Appendix A contains portions of the National Restaurant Association's *Safety Self-Inspection Program for Food Service Operators,* a handy guide for checking on OSHA compliance and safe conditions for the public.

Most accidents in public areas employing dining room personnel involve falls and strains caused by improper lifting. Falls are often the result of wet floors, debris on the floor, obstacles in main traffic aisles, and loose or torn carpets. These areas should be included in the supervisor's inspection check list. However, surveillance should not be limited to the preopening inspection. A potential hazard may develop at any time and must be removed at once.

Fire Safety

If you had a fire, could your guests and staff get out of the building safely? Fire safety ordinances have come a long way since the disastrous Cocoanut Grove fire in 1942 took 491 lives; yet in June 1977, 160 people died and more than a hundred were injured in a Kentucky supper club fire. As in many other fatal fires, most of the deaths were caused by smoke inhalation, not burns.

Seeing that fire exits are kept clear is not enough. In the Kentucky fire, no negligence was reported. Yet there was a large loss of life because people could not find the exits. Other factors in fire-related injuries and deaths include overcrowding of the premises, blocked exits, and panic among the patrons—all of which can be prevented by a trained, fire-conscious staff. Periodic fire drills should be scheduled with the staff so that in the event of an emergency, they will be able to assist guests in vacating the building.

EEOC and Other Federal Regulations

Those pertaining to dining room operations have to do mostly with employment and hiring practices. They are discussed in later chapters.

Liquor Laws

A liquor license is one of the most valuable assets a restaurant can have. Loss of that license for violation of liquor laws can be very costly. Even more costly these days is *third party liability*. If you serve a customer who is obviously intoxicated (a violation of the law, to begin with) and he goes out and smashes into someone on the highway, you may be sued by the victim or by his heirs as a contributor or third party to the accident. In one such case, a judgment was made against a California bar for $1.9 million. While most restaurants carry liability insurance (and some states require that restaurants and taverns carry special "dram shop" coverage), you have no defense and cannot collect from the insurance company if you are in violation of the law.

Hospitality Magazine offers advice to prevent such suits. If a customer is *obviously intoxicated* (O.I.), do the following:[1]

> Risk a possible $100 fine for refusing to serve him/her. It may save you from a $1-million third party injury suit. Don't try to physically restrain a violent patron. Document that you verbally tried to prevent him/her from leaving your premises in his/her car, and that he/she was refused liquor service.
>
> Instruct employees to call your manager to make decisions on patron problems. It is his/her responsibility. When a management decision is made, document it. Identify employees who were participants, or witnesses to what you did. Take employees' statements in writing. Record driver's license and Social Security number, and ask names and addresses of relatives or closest friends, who may help you locate them two years from now when, no longer in your employ, they may be needed to testify about the incident which suddenly has become a third party damage suit.
>
> Educate employees to be alert to any unusual behavior of a patron, possibly suggesting O.I. Urge them to try to remember the patron's appearance, speech, and when and where he/she attracted attention. Waitresses should converse with suspect patrons, try to recognize when they have reached the state of "obviousness." Train your doorman or maître d' to be alert to anyone seeking to enter your premises intoxicated. (In California it is not against the law to get drunk in an establishment. But it is against the law to allow customers to enter or leave while intoxicated.)
>
> Check your insurance. Know whether your liability protection covers you both on and off your premises. Be absolutely sure of the

---

[1]Reprinted from *Restaurant Hospitality*, March, 1977.

validity of an ID card. Treat the card as if the patron were using it to cash a $500 check.

The restaurant industry still has no sure-fire protection against third party damage action, and that liability insurance is becoming harder and harder to buy. Probably the best "insurance" is education of employees in dealing with O.I.'s, and written documentation of how they handled an obviously drunk customer. Documentation may very well prove to be the restaurant owner's case-winning evidence in court.

Following these practices also helps to protect the restaurant from fines or loss of license from liquor law violations. However, there are other aspects of liquor law that you must comply with. You should know what the law says about your type of license. For example, it may restrict the legal hours of service; specify who may serve alcoholic beverages; and regulate types of advertising, merchandising, promotions, and giveaways. Each state has its own laws, and you should obtain a copy.

Sanitation

We tend to think of sanitation and health inspections as involving only the back of the house. However, they affect the front of the house as well. It is the front that the guest sees. He must draw his conclusions about the cleanliness of the kitchen and the safety of the food from the conditions and practices he sees in the dining rooms and public areas of the establishment, especially the rest rooms.

Areas of primary concern to the dining room manager are personal cleanliness of the staff, including clothing and bodily cleanliness, use of hairnets or caps, and absence of communicable diseases; food and equipment handling practices, such as the use of tongs, forks, and spoons to dish up food; handling sanitized silverware by the handles and not by the eating ends; proper handling of ice to prevent contamination; proper storage of food used by the dining room staff, such as sugar and other condiments; cleanliness of rest room facilities; and general housekeeping. If there are any refrigeration units in the dining area, they must be maintained at the proper temperatures.

Appendix B contains a portion of the National Restaurant Association's *Self-Inspection Program for Food Service Operators on Sanitation and Safe Food Handling.* Like the safety self-inspection, it is a handy management tool.

Consumer Protection Legislation

At this time, consumer protection legislation is quite new and exists only in some local jurisdictions. Whether or not the antismoking supporters will gain wide support is hard to say. Truth-in-menu, however, should be standard operating procedure for any business, regardless of whether the law is passed. It makes no sense to falsely promote an item. Saying that your fish is fresh when it is frozen or that your meat is prime when it isn't only raises false expectations in the guest. Then you have a dissatisfied customer.

W. Michael O'Neal, president of the New York State Restaurant Association, offers these guidelines from *Metropolitan Restaurant News.*

It must be understood that there are certain areas that cause the greatest concern to consumer groups and government agencies who are responsible for pure food laws and other such type of regulations. For example: food is considered adulterated if any of the following conditions exist:

1. If any valuable constituent has been in whole or in part omitted therefrom.
2. If any substance is used to replace the product either in part or wholly.
3. If the product is damaged or inferior and this fact has been concealed.
4. If any substance (not seasoning) has been added or mixed so as to increase the weight, diminish the quality or make it appear better than it is.

In the area of misrepresentation, the four following items seem to be the most common:

1. Quality or grade products misrepresented.
2. Point of origin of food products not as advertised.
3. The size, weight or portion not as advertised.
4. Frozen, canned or preserved products advertised as fresh.

The above-mentioned are a summary of the areas in which menu descriptions arise. Remember, accuracy in menu also includes oral descriptions by the employees.

It is illegal to use the terminology "homemade" in New York State; "homestyle," "made on premises," "our own recipe" are all acceptable substitutions. If the word "fresh" were to appear in front of shrimp cocktail you might be asked if they were actually fresh or frozen. If they were at one time frozen you should change the word fresh to chilled, iced or simply shrimp cocktail.

Preventing Civil Law Suits

Prevention of accidents that could lead to law suits and negligence claims is part of the supervisor's job. Another type of claim is for physical assault or verbal abuse by an employee or another person. The courts have held that a restaurant keeper has a duty to provide protection to his patrons from insult or annoyance while they are in his restaurant. To put a stop to such annoyance, he may eject the person guilty of the offense. As for protection from assaults, the courts have required that all reasonable care be taken to prevent such assaults. Certainly this includes careful screening of employees hired to work in contact with the public. Any employee who cannot curb either his fists or his tongue should not be permitted to work in a dining room.

Dealing with a guest you suspect of stealing is very touchy. Do not make accusations. Raise questions until you are absolutely sure and have proof to press charges.

In any case, whether it be an accident or other type of incident, be sure you record all the details in your logbook. Be very specific as to who was involved, who said what to whom, when and where it happened, and what conditions existed at the time. Such a record could be invaluable in the event of a law suit.

Chapter 6

Merchandising and Sales Promotion

Developing an overall merchandising and sales program for a restaurant is the responsibility of management. Because the dining room manager is in daily contact with the customers, his suggestions will probably be sought on those aspects of merchandising related to dining room operations.

Once the merchandising program is developed, the dining room manager is responsible for carrying out his part of the program. This may include training the staff in salesmanship, special service techniques, internal advertising materials and point of sales displays, and promotional giveaways.

Selling and service techniques were discussed briefly in Chap. 4 as part of the standards of service. They must be incorporated into the steps of service.

Salesmanship

The professional waiter and waitress are not just order-takers and carriers of trays. First and foremost, they must be salesmen. Their function is not only to get the customer served today, but also to get that customer to return again ... and again. While that guest is in the restaurant, the salesman-waiter can suggest items that will increase the guest's enjoyment of his meal, increase the restaurant's sales, and increase the waiter's tips.

The first rule of salesmanship is *know your product*. In a restaurant this means that the service staff must know the menu items, as well as the major ingredients and the method of preparation. If wines are sold, the staff should know the wine list thoroughly (see Fig. 6.1). Most important, they should know what the food items and wines taste like. It is difficult to be an enthusiastic salesman for something you have never tasted. The cost of food and wines used for periodic tasting and training sessions is a small investment that should produce large returns. (Incidentally, the service staff is often a good taste panel for evaluating new recipes.)

Fig. 6.1. Merchandising wines at Cellar in the Sky. (*Courtesy* of Windows on the World, Inhilco, and Ezra Stoller.)

The second rule of selling is *know your customer*. If at all possible, know his name and address him by it. That is basic human relations. In restaurants where customers make reservations, the guest identifies himself when he arrives. From then on, it should be easy for the staff to continue addressing him by name. The maître d' or seating host can copy the guest's name onto a small piece of paper, along with the number of the assigned table. When he seats the party, he discreetly gives the slip to the captain or waiter. In hotel dining rooms, conference guests and conventioneers make the task easy by wearing badges or name tags. Some discretion is necessary, however, if the name tags give only first names. Not everyone likes to be addressed familiarly by people they don't know.

In informal, fast turnover restaurants, it becomes a bit more difficult to learn guests' names, but it still can be done. The host certainly should know who his regular customers are, and he can pass their names along to the waiter or waitress serving them. Among young people it is the fashion these days to wear their names or nicknames on their clothing. Young people, as well as adults, like to be called by name.

However, salesmanship goes beyond knowing your customer's name. It includes knowing his tastes and preferences. In a restaurant with a large amount of repeat business from a regular clientele, the staff usually learns the tastes and preferences of the regulars. Where there is a large transient clientele, it becomes more difficult but not impossible. An observant waiter who pays attention to his guests can learn a great deal about their tastes and preferences by the things they order and the way they order. This does not involve prying or eavesdropping, just paying attention to what the guests are saying when they give their orders.

The self-assured guest who knows exactly what he wants and orders a complete meal without any suggestion from the waiter needs no selling; he has already sold himself. The waiter-salesman then concentrates on providing the best service to sell this guest on coming back again. The guest who hesitates or asks questions will appreciate suggestions from the waiter. Some may just want to be reassured that the item they have selected is a good choice. Others want to be guided in their selection. These guests are most likely to make impulse sales if positive suggestive selling techniques are used.

The third rule of selling is *match the product to the customer's needs or preferences*. True salesmanship is not just hard selling to push volume sales. Rather, it is matching what you have to sell with what the customer wants to buy. In the restaurant, the waiter-salesman must match his menu to the customer's tastes and preferences and then make selling suggestions that will get a positive response. A steak-and-potatoes guest may be receptive to a suggestion of shrimp cocktail or apple pie a la mode. A lady who is dieting will not appreciate being tempted with a hot fudge sundae or a rich pastry, though she may be very receptive to a dish of fresh strawberries or melon for dessert. The high protein dieter could be interested in a selection of cheeses instead of a dessert. For the anniversary couple, you may suggest a bottle of champagne; and for the executive with an expense account, a cognac after dinner and a good cigar.

Salesmanship is not limited to the more elegant restaurants. In moderately priced coffee shops, selling suggestions by the service staff can increase sales of first courses and desserts as well as side orders such as salads, french fries, and large size drinks.

The fourth rule of selling is *don't promote it if you can't produce it*. In dining room selling, this means that the service staff must have up-to-the-minute information about the availability of each menu item and know which items are running low.

Along the same line is a corollary rule *give good service*. People expect good service when they go out to eat. If expectations are built up for a great meal, great service, and a great experience, the letdown will be twice as great if these things fail to materialize.

The fifth rule of selling is *be positive and enthusiastic*. How many desserts do you think have been sold with this line: "You don't want any dessert, do you?" Not many. "Any dessert here?" is not much better. Try this: "Are you folks ready for dessert? We have some terrific strawberry whipped cream pie tonight." When the guest asks, "How's the seafood plate?" he's fishing for reassurance. A lukewarm response such as "It's OK" does nothing for him or for the average check. Try instead: "It's very good, but we have an excellent fried fish combination plate on the complete dinner. You get soup, dessert, and our special house salad with it." Never run down an item, just suggest something better.

The sixth rule of selling is *say thank you*. By showing appreciation for his business, you are recognizing that he is doing you a favor; you are not doing a favor by serving him. When you show him that you value his patronage, you are much more likely to get his business in the future.

The last rule of selling is *know when to quit*. If the guest is not receptive this time, he may be next time. If you push too hard, you may not get a next time.

Service Techniques

An eye-catching presentation of a specialty menu item can increase impulse sales of that item and create an image and reputation for the restaurant. The item need not be exotic, but it should be profitable.

For many years The Pump Room in Chicago was one of the most famous restaurants in the country. Part of its fame was built on showmanship in the dining room. Food was carried with a flourish into the room on flaming swords, and coffee was served by a coffee boy costumed in oriental dress and feathered turban.

In another Chicago restaurant, Don Roth's Blackhawk, the salad is dressed at tableside in spinning salad bowls. The technique is very simple—a round metal bowl set in a bed of crushed ice. It is the waiter's recitation as he spins the bowl and mixes the salad that makes the show.

Showmanship is not limited to luxury restaurants. Moderately priced steak houses create a show with salad displays and sizzle platters that give the service sound as well as visual appeal. Other techniques include carving wagons, dessert carts, salad buffets, specialty servers such as roll girls, relish tray service, and cordial wagons.

Maintaining the Image

The dining room manager does not usually make the final decisions as to what the presentation items will be. However, he is responsible for carrying out the service. If the menu items are changed frequently, he must check with the chef to find out which items are to be featured and how they are to be presented (portions, garnitures, and so forth).

It is the manager's responsibility to see that the presentation is maintained, that the service personnel do not become stale or sloppy in their presentation, that the dessert cart and salad bar are kept supplied and immaculate, that carving wagons are kept neat and orderly and hot, that specialty servers do not neglect any tables, and that cordials are presented at the right time and with glassware sparkling. Any presentation that is not maintained from first party to last can turn off the guests, not tempt them.

Another aspect of merchandising is garniture and food presentation. In many restaurants the servers must add the garnishes to the food and drinks they serve. They may have to dish up some of the items as well. Proper plating and garnishing are part of the merchandising program. A tired, limp sprig of parsley plopped on a plate does nothing to enhance the appeal of the dish. People eat with their eyes. If the food is presented in a messy or casual way, the appeal is lost.

Sometimes a presentation is strictly for display, such as an exhibit of wines. This kind of display must also be maintained to keep its appeal fresh. It is amazing how quickly the dust can gather and take the sheen off the most attractive display. A dusty wine glass sells no wine!

Internal Advertising Materials

The most important piece of internal promotional material in the restaurant is the menu. Usually a great deal of planning and thought go into the layout and printing of a menu to make it an effective selling tool. The dining room manager may or may not have participated in the planning process, but he definitely is responsible for the upkeep and appearance of menus presented to guests.

No self-respecting salesman would present a soiled, dog-eared piece of sales literature to a prospective customer, neither should the restaurant sales staff. Dirty, torn menus imply a dirty, sloppily run business and negate all the effort that has gone into building the public image of the restaurant just to save a few pennies on menu printing.

Equally self-defeating is the negative effect of menus with price increases penciled in. The customer is immediately confronted with the fact that he is going to get less for his money. The small cost of printing new menus when prices must be increased is an unavoidable business expense.

Guests sometimes ask for a menu to take home. Unless the menu is printed in gold on platinum, give it to them. It is the best (and usually the cheapest) kind of advertising a restaurant can have. If the menus are very expensive, have some less expensive souvenir menus printed to give away, and be sure the name of the restaurant, the full address, and the telephone number are prominently shown.

Operators who give out souvenir menus usually have them printed without prices. In that way, a larger printing can be ordered to reduce the cost per menu. It also solves the negative image problem when raising prices.

POS—Point-of-Sale Promotion

Some restaurant operators are borrowing a technique from retailers and using POS promotional material such as table tents, signs, posters, streamers or banners, menu clip-ons, placemats, and hats or buttons for the staff—all carrying some special promotional theme or message. The purpose is to produce an extra sale from the customer once he is in the store. In the restaurant, the promotion may be aimed at an additional sale or at switching the guest from a standard, low profit item to a featured high profit item.

Here again, it is the dining room manager's responsibility to see that the promotional program is carried out—that buttons are worn, that table tents are put out on every table, and that posters are displayed. Where the promotion is primarily in-house (as opposed to external advertising), the success of the promotion depends primarily on the dining room manager. He is in an excellent position to make a strong impact on sales; and his staff is in a good position to benefit from increased tips. Thus special promotions benefit employees as well as the restaurant owner.

Premiums and Giveaways

Some special promotions include giving away premiums with the purchase of a particular item. The giveaway may be glassware, coffee mugs, or teapots. This type of promotion is usually limited to fast turnover, high-volume operations, although specialty cocktail lounges may use premiums occasionally. Generally, however, they are used only in highly competitive situations because they create problems of maintaining inventories. Giveaways can also be costly and can interfere with the flow of service.

Another type of giveaway is used by higher-priced restaurants; some small favor, usually in keeping with the theme of the restaurant, is given to all guests during the course of the service. Here again the presentation must be built into the steps of service, and the dining room manager must control the supply of these items.

Family-type restaurants often have small favors for children—a special comic book about the restaurant, a menu that becomes a hat to take home, a placemat to crayon, or a treasure chest of inexpensive toys from which the child can choose.

Premiums for adults may include small flowers or leis for the ladies and cigars for the men. A western theme restaurant presents chocolate candies wrapped as gold coins; a Polynesian restaurant gives flower leis to both men and women. A continental restaurant gives an after dinner cordial to each adult guest. (Local liquor laws should be consulted before giving alcoholic beverages gratis; some state liquor laws do not allow it.)

Pump Priming

The owner of a medium-priced restaurant says: "See that big corner booth in the back? I try to get a group in there early in the evening, especially a gang that's out to celebrate. Then, I've got this gimmick. It's called a Yard of Ale. At the right time, I buy a round for the booth. The waiters make a big production out of carrying those crazy glasses through the dining room, and the bunch in the booth think it's really great. Then I start selling yards of ale all over the room, and it goes on all night. As soon as people see them, they want them. I make a terrific markup on them, and the giveaway costs me peanuts."

Pump priming, that is, giving away a small amount of food or drink in order to stimulate impulse sales, can be effective for certain types of items. Generally the items must be highly visible, even theatrical, in their presentation. The technique is most effective in occasion-type restaurants where people are out for a show as well as a meal.

Chapter 7

Meeting the Public

So far we have discussed the technical aspects of dining room operation. Let's get the guest back into proper perspective. Too often the service staff can become so wrapped up in the technical aspects of service that the guest becomes "the chicken potpie on table 22" instead of a human being. When the employees are thinking of the customers as a hindrance to their work instead of the very reason that their jobs exist, something is very wrong.

Satisfying Needs and Expectations

The restaurant business is a people business. We must satisfy the customer's needs today if we are to get his business tomorrow; and we need his business tomorrow if we are to stay in business.

How do we satisfy his needs? Behavioral scientists tell us that need satisfaction is the basis of all human behavior. Some needs may be obvious, but many are obscure. Abraham Maslow, the noted psychologist, proposed a hierarchy of needs. At the lowest level are physiological needs such as food, air, and shelter. Next are security needs—safety and freedom from fear. At the third and fourth levels are social needs—love and group belonging—and status needs—prestige and rank. At the top of Maslow's hierarchy is what he calls self-actualization, that is, the need to develop one's self and to use one's maximum potential.

There are other theories of human behavior, but Maslow's need hierarchy is useful to explain what people really want when they go out to dine.

At the physiological need level, the guest is in search of food to satisfy his hunger. But he can satisfy that need at any restaurant in town as well as in his own home. Why should he satisfy it at your restaurant?

Perhaps it is because you satisfy his needs at the next level—security or freedom from fear. Security is both physical and psychological. The guest wants to know that the food he eats is safe and that the rest rooms are clean. Also at this level is freedom from being robbed, a fear held by many who don't want to go into unsafe neighborhoods at night. A safe, well-lit parking lot may be needed if your guests feel threatened. Psychological security may be an even more important factor in dining out. For years restaurants had a public image of being haughty and snobbish, scaring off many patrons who were afraid they would be insulted by a head waiter or made to look foolish. In this instance, the ego is more fragile than the body.

Psychological security may be obtained by just recognizing a person's presence. When you ignore a guest, you are denying his very existence and posing the ultimate threat to his ego. Recognition need not be a noisy demonstrative welcome. It can simply be a smile and a "good evening." The host at the door may be taking a telephone reservation, but he can still acknowledge the arriving couple with a smile and a nod. Eye contact is a very powerful way of communicating. Another handy communication device is the little phrase "for you" as in "I will be happy to check on that wine *for you.*"

At the next level on the hierarchy are social needs—group belonging and acceptance. What makes a guest become a regular? Probably a major factor is that he feels at home. He knows the staff and feels accepted and welcome. He belongs.

Next on Maslow's hierarchy are status needs—prestige and rank. Satisfying guests' needs at this level ought to be duck soup for the professional dining room staff. Could a woman leave your restaurant and exclaim, "The service was great; I feel like a queen"? Or could a man say, "Boy, they really treated me like a big shot"?

At the top of the need hierarchy is self-actualization. The restaurant patron striving to satisfy this need is often searching for the gourmet experience, for the ultimate wine or cheese or the latest 'in' place to add to his roster of experiences.

In addition to his collection of needs, the guest has a set of expectations that must be fulfilled. If they are not, he will have a bad response regardless of the quality of food or service. Expectations may be based on past experience at a restaurant, recommendations of friends, advertising, or just general ideas about dining out. If these expectations are not fulfilled, he will leave dissatisfied.

Furthermore, when the guest walks in the door, he comes from some place, some activity, and some experience. This experience may have been pleasant or unpleasant. He may have had an argument with the boss, a traffic ticket along the way, or lost out on a big sale. The female guest may have spent the day with squabbling youngsters or on the job with an aggravating boss or client. Perhaps she just spent a half-hour looking for a parking space. We don't know what situation the guest has come from when he enters our door. We have to take him the way he comes, with all his needs, moods, and expectations.

There is a quality that professional service personnel should cultivate in themselves to enable them to deal with the unpredictable nature of the guest. It is the quality of *empathy* or the ability to put yourself in the other person's shoes and know what he is feeling. The person with empathy understands the embarrassment of an unsteady elderly person who has spilled something, the dismay of an inexperienced diner who ordered an unfamiliar dish he discovers he doesn't like, and the nervousness of a young man trying to impress an important date.

In business we say that this is a customer-oriented approach. It is based on the recognition that the customer is the reason we are in business and that each customer's patronage is essential to the continuance of the business. This customer-orientation does not just happen. Management and supervisors must put the customer first and devote considerable time and effort to staff training. We will have more to say on this important subject in Chap. 11.

Handling Complaints

In the past, many successful businessmen instilled a customer-oriented attitude in their employees with the slogan *the customer is always right*. A more modern version recognizes that employees have minds of their own. *The customer may not always be right, but he is never wrong*. The more enlightened approach eliminates the question of whether the customer is right or wrong because it doesn't matter. The object is to retain his goodwill and future business. *Never let a dissatisfied customer leave the restaurant*.

Another customer-oriented approach is *you never win an argument with a customer* because if you win, you lose his future business, and there are very few restaurant operations that can afford to lose customers. Actually, the guest who complains is doing you a favor. First, he is giving you a chance to correct something that dissatisfied him. Second, he is alerting you to a situation that may have dissatisfied other guests as well. Many people will not complain; they just won't come back. And they may tell their friends about their unhappy experience. In that case, you won't see those people either. Word-of-mouth can be a very strong influence on sales, either positive or negative.

Every guest complaint should be seen as valid, regardless of whether you think it is justified or not. Obviously, the guest thinks it is valid, and he is the one who is paying the tab. Telling the guest that "nobody ever complained about that dish before" is telling him that he doesn't know what is good or that his taster is out of whack. Let's face it, everyone who eats food is an expert on good food, at least in his own eyes. Perhaps no one ever did complain about the particular dish. There is always a first time. Even in the best run kitchens there is always a possibility of human error. Do not assume that your kitchen is always perfect.

Offering excuses or attempting to blame someone else are other unprofessional responses to complaints. The complaining guest is not interested in explanations or blame placing. He is only interested in having the situation corrected. The woman who found a fly in her mornay sauce does not care to hear a long description of your pest control procedures. She only wants the offending dish replaced. The man who is unhappy about slow service isn't interested in knowing that you are three people short today or that the boss is cutting back on the payroll. He has his own problems, and he doesn't want to hear about yours. He came to dinner to get away from problems for a little while, and he wants the service he is paying for.

Most guest complaints can be resolved with an apology and a corrective action by the supervisor or waiter. It may mean getting help for a waiter who is stuck, correcting a fault with a dish, or offering a replacement. If the complaint is of a nature that it can't be made right, you can show the guest that you really care about his patronage by picking up all or part of the check or by offering a free drink, dessert, or a bottle of wine. If the guest is ready to depart or is calling or writing to complain after the experience, you may ask him for another chance and offer a meal on the house (depending on the house policy, of course). Whatever the action, apologize and mean it.

Fortunately, frauds, professional cheats, and chronic complainers are few in number. Giving a free meal or drink to a professional cheat once in a while is much less costly than losing the future business of a guest with a legitimate complaint.

Occasionally a waiter may see a complaining guest as a threat—an insult to his ability to do his job, or perhaps even a threat to his personal integrity. Admittedly, there are people in this world who feel inadequate and insecure. They sometimes try to compensate by bullying people who are not in a position to fight back. These types are a real challenge, and that is the only way to deal with them ... as a challenge to your professionalism. Lowering yourself to their level by acting defensively is just what they want you to do. Once you permit yourself to get angry with them, you have lost control of the situation. Your objective is to keep in control by providing every service necessary to satisfy them. Give them extra attention to be sure they have absolutely nothing to complain about. Sometimes the insecure, complaining guest can be won over to become a steady guest and a loyal supporter once he learns to feel secure in your restaurant and knows he will receive all the attention he craves.

Chapter 8

The Basics of Supervision

The professional dining room manager's biggest job is dealing with people—the guests he serves and the staff who provide this service. Although the various types of service require varying degrees of technical skills, the most important skill a dining room manager can have is the ability to deal with people. This chapter and the following one discuss the basic principles of supervision and motivation. These skills are important in dealing with employees.

What Is Supervision?

It is often defined as "getting work done through people," but that is a bit oversimplified. Supervision is

1. Seeing that work gets done
2. Seeing that the work meets standards set by management
3. Seeing that the work is done as efficiently as possible
4. Seeing that the work is done in accordance with the policies practices set by management
5. Being held accountable or responsible for the results, day in and out

"Seeing that work gets done" is another oversimplificat involves a number of activities.

1. Deciding what work is to be done
2. Dividing the work into specific tasks
3. Deciding how the tasks are to be performed—that is, the s that must be met
4. Obtaining any materials or equipment needed to perform
5. Obtaining any information that may be needed to perform
6. Assigning the tasks to specific workers

59

7. Instructing them in what the task is and how it is to be performed
8. Observing to be sure the task is performed according to instructions
9. Determining the cause of any substandard performance and taking corrective action if necessary

This list may seem a bit abstract. Let's see how it fits the job of the dining room supervisor.

First, what is the work that must be done? Customers must be served in the dining room seven days a week for breakfast, lunch, and dinner. The work may be classified as serving and clearing tables. The dining room manager determines the number of workers needed for each shift to serve the number of guests anticipated. Work may further be subdivided by dividing the tables into stations. Side duties such as stocking side stands and dining room housekeeping chores may be identified. Once these divisions of work are determined, they are assigned to the staff by means of the schedule. The dining room supervisor is also responsible for seeing that there is an adequate supply of linen, china, silverware, menus, and other equipment necessary to operate his room. He may be directly responsible for ordering the supplies and putting them into service, or his responsibility may end when he reports his needs to the manager. The supervisor must also keep informed about the activities of the other departments in the restaurant and about conditions outside that could affect his business. One specific type of information that he must provide to his staff daily is menu changes.

Staff instruction may consist of special instructions for a job that is to be performed once such as a special service for a particular customer, a review of a new menu, demonstration of a particular procedure with the entire staff at a staff meeting, or a series of training sessions for a new employee.

During service the dining room supervisor is alert to the progress of service at each table in the dining room. He notes any lapse in service and receives customer complaints. Afterward he finds out why the lapse occurred and takes steps to prevent it from happening again. He may correct an individual employee, review a procedure with the entire staff, or work with the chef or kitchen manager to improve coordination between the dining room and the kitchen.

The preceding description gives a more accurate view of "getting the work done through people." There are several other aspects of supervision that must be emphasized. First, the supervisor must be willing to accept the responsibility for the operation of his department. As Harry Truman put it, "The buck stops here." When the performance of the department is not acceptable, the supervisor takes action to bring it to standard. Second, the supervisor represents the management to the staff and to the public. He must be knowledgeable in the employment

policies and practices of the house and be prepared to carry them out. Similarly, he must know the house policies regarding the handling of the public, such as when to "comp" a check, how to handle a complaint, and how to deal with an inebriated guest. Third, the supervisor also represents the staff to management. He must be aware of what his staff personnel are thinking and feeling about their job situation, and he must be able to communicate the staff morale to management. Fourth, the function of supervision is continuous. It is not a job that ends with the completion of a task or assignment. There is always the performance of work to be overseen, corrected, and planned for. The supervisor's job is never done.

Authority and Responsibility

In the preceding section we used the word *responsible*. By accepting responsibility, the supervisor assumes an obligation to perform certain functions; that is, he will see that the department operates in a certain way. If he does not carry out this obligation, the department will not function effectively and efficiently. Some of the dining room manager's specific responsibilities include the following:

1. Enforcing the policies and standards set by management (Policies and standards will be defined below.)
2. Seeing that the desired quality of service is given
3. Seeing that the operations in his department comply with all applicable laws (including labor laws, liquor laws if applicable, consumer protection laws, and so forth)
4. Maintaining safe conditions for both guests and employees
5. Controlling costs within his department and protecting the property of the company
6. Generating sales to the extent possible in his position

The other side of the coin is authority. In order to fulfill his obligation, the supervisor must be able to make certain decisions and carry them out without asking the permission of his superior. Management delegates (gives to him) certain authority, the right to make certain types of decisions necessary in the operation of the department.

Policy and Standards

In some cases, management may not wish to delegate complete authority. If they did, each department head would make independent decisions, and there would be no continuity between departments. When similar types of decisions are involved, management writes a policy. This is a guideline for handling such decisions so that the same decision is reached in each department when similar situations arise. For example, a personnel policy might state, "Each employee is entitled to two weeks vacation with pay after one year's employment."

Another area in which management will not wish to delegate complete authority is in the desired level of performance. Management will establish standards that each department must meet. These may be cost standards (linen cost should not exceed $.XX per cover served), productivity standards (dining room staff productivity goal is XXX covers per manhour), or performance standards (orders shall be taken within XX minutes of seating the guest).

In large companies, standards are usually well defined and written down. Supervisors and managers are measured by how well their departments meet these standards.

In small businesses or individual restaurants, the standards may not be well defined or written down, but they still exist in the mind of the owner or manager. The dining room supervisor must try to interpret the level of performance desired or substitute his own standards.

Leadership

So far we have described what a supervisor does. How he does it may be called his leadership style. Behavioral scientists have identified four types of leaders: authoritarian, paternalistic, democratic, and participative.

Sometimes we find a fifth type—abdicative. The abdicative leader is really a nonleader. He lets his staff make the daily decisions about when and how they shall work. However, this does not mean the abdicative leader is idle. In fact, he may be the busiest person in the dining room— bustling about, bussing tables, serving coffee, and fetching silverware from the kitchen. This is a highly paid busboy rather than a true leader who gets the work done *through other people*.

The Authoritarian Leader

This type of leader is sometimes called an autocrat. He is the I-am-the-boss type. He makes all decisions arbitrarily without consulting anyone for information or opinions on the matter. He demands total obedience to his orders. He usually considers the employees greatly inferior to himself, assuming they are motivated only for their own personal gain and not interested in the requirements of the company or the job. He believes that people will do what he wants them to do only by fear of punishment. The authoritarian leader is often concerned with preserving his authority and administering discipline to those who do not obey his orders.

Paternalistic Leader

This is the father-knows-best type of leader. He differs from the authoritarian in that he cares about the welfare of the staff and wants them to be happy. The price he asks in return is that they accept all his decisions without question. He still does not value any contribution they may wish to make since he assumes they aren't competent enough to make contributions. He may select certain individuals to be groomed for management, but he probably does not permit even them to contribute very much. He may provide a considerable amount of employee benefits, pay high wages, and offer good working conditions. However, they are all given by him unilaterally, with no participation in the planning or operation by the recipients of his gifts.

The Democratic Leader and the Participative Leader

The democratic leader identifies problems and refers them to his group to resolve by vote of the majority. This type of leader is usually much more successful than the autocrat or the paternalist in getting people to work for him. He involves the group in decisions that affect them. The problem with this type of leadership is that what the majority chooses to do may not be in the best interest of the business.

The participative style of leadership is getting much attention in the business press at present. The participative leader says to his subordinates, "Here is what has to be done. Tell me how you plan to do it. If it does not conflict with the policies and objectives of the company, you may go ahead and do what you propose. Furthermore, I will evaluate you on how well you achieve your own plan." This type of leadership may be more suited to supervision of managerial or professional level employees than to workers doing routine tasks, but the basic principles of participation and involvement of the individual are still applicable.

The Supervisor's Responsibilities to the Staff

One supervisor says, "I believe I have certain responsibilities to my staff. If I don't fulfill those responsibilities, the department will look bad, and then I will look bad. It's strictly a matter of enlightened self-interest." These are the responsibilities this supervisor has to his staff.

1. To give people complete instructions and guidance on what is expected of them
2. To provide a safe, clean working environment
3. To have available the equipment and material people need to do their jobs
4. To give a fair hearing to their suggestions and complaints

5. To correct any work performance that is not meeting standards (It is unfair to those who are doing good work to tolerate substandard performance in others.)
6. To recognize good performance and let the employee know where he stands
7. To have personal respect for the dignity of each individual
8. To be fair in making judgments and enforcing rules and regulations
9. To understand that workers have a life outside of work, that their values and priorities may not be the same as the boss's, and that they are not available on demand to do the boss's bidding
10. To see that all members of the staff are paid a fair and living wage

Discipline Versus Corrective Action

Discipline is often thought of as punishment for past behavior. The parent punishes the child to impress on him that certain behavior is bad and must not be repeated in the future. Unfortunately, on-the-job discipline can sometimes be revenge for past behavior rather than prevention of certain future behavior.

What we are really concerned with is corrective action, the last step in the sequence of activities (p. 60) that constitute supervision. The object is to motivate the individual to a desirable performance in the future, regardless of past performance. Vindictive disciplinary action by the supervisor is more likely to cause resentment and a negative response.

To correct undesirable behavior, the supervisor must first discuss the situation privately with the individual and listen to his side of the story. There may be circumstances that make a disciplinary action inappropriate. An infraction of a rule may have been unintentional or the result of a misunderstanding. Poor work performance may indicate a need for additional training rather than a reprimand.

When criticism or a reprimand is in order, it should be given in a positive manner. Correct the specific behavior, not the person. Give him a chance to save face and maintain his dignity. Destroying a person's self-respect and confidence will not improve his work performance. Obviously this means having your talk in private, in an environment free of interruption. It also means treating the matter as completely confidential. Don't just chew out the individual on the fly. Be specific about the behavior that prompted your action. Be sure you handle his situation exactly the same as you would handle it with another person. Whether the staff is unionized or not, make a written record of your warning with the particulars and send a copy to the office to be put in the personnel files. You should also note it in your logbook.

Usually one interview is enough to resolve the situation. However, if the behavior is repeated, further action is required. The group-oriented leader will try to give every benefit of the doubt to the employee. He asks himself whether he made the situation absolutely clear to the employee. Could he have misunderstood the last conversation? Is there a language problem? It may be that the individual is just in the wrong job. Some people are just not comfortable in dealing with the public but can work well in back of the house. Others may not be able to deal with the stress of a rush period and need a more even-paced work environment.

Labor turnover is very costly in any organization. Throwing people out like tissues destroys the morale of those who remain. If an employee thinks he might get the ax tomorrow, he is not motivated to top performance today. A competent, skilled employee will decide to take his chances elsewhere rather than risk being fired. The supervisor who has a high turnover among his staff is probably doing something wrong.

Chapter 9

Motivation

The *how* of getting work done is really getting people to do the work. This is best accomplished by getting them to want to do the work. In other words, they must be motivated.

Motivation is not manipulation. Motivation is providing a means of satisfying the individual's needs in a way that fills the needs of the business as well. The manipulator is only concerned with getting people to behave in a way that satisfies his own needs without regard for the other person's needs or interests.

Let's look at the individual we want to motivate—the employee. He is not an automaton. He is a total person, an individual with many parts to his being.

- Physical health
- Mental health
- Emotional health
- Educational background
- Home life and family
- Financial status
- Religious, moral, and social values
- Personality
- Career or job expectations
- Hobbies and interests
- Future expectations
- Abilities and skills

The supervisor must deal with the total person and with the wants and needs created by all the aspects of his being.

In Chap. 7 we described Maslow's hierarchy of needs. It represents one way of understanding human behavior. How does this theory apply to people on the job? First of all, most people work for one primary reason—to make a living; that is, to satisfy their physiological needs by providing food, shelter, and clothing for themselves and their families. Where they work, what they work at, and how they work are factors in higher level need satisfaction. Once an individual is earning a wage adequate to provide him with the necessities, his basic needs are satisfied (although for reasons of status or self-actualization he may wish to satisfy his housing, food, and clothing needs on a higher, more expensive level).

Once a person's physiological needs are met, he moves on to the next level—security and freedom from fear. This is a need that motivates people to join unions for job security and to obtain benefits such as sick pay and health insurance.

The next level on the need hierarchy is love, belonging, and group acceptance. Peer group acceptance is a very powerful need, and it cannot be satisfied by management. Every work group forms its own peer structure with its own leader. Knowing who the peer leader is and winning his support can be effective in winning support from the total group.

Management can appeal to belonging needs by including employees in the decision-making process and keeping them informed of developments in the company. Participation and sharing of information are effective in building a spirit of cooperation and team work, which is what belonging is all about.

The need for prestige and status is fairly well recognized in business. Among hourly employees, recognition through gifts (such as pins or tie clasps for length of service), write-ups in the company paper of achievements on and off the job, and promotion of qualified employees to higher level positions are common practices.

Recognition of good performance is always rated highly when workers are asked what they want from their jobs. It is also one of the easiest (and least expensive) needs for the company to meet. Unfortunately, managers often forget that the most effective form of recognition is a few words of approval and appreciation for a job well done.

At the top of the need hierarchy is self-realization, the need to develop one's potential to its fullest and to use one's skills and abilities. One attribute is pride of workmanship. Everyone wants the satisfaction of knowing he does his job well. The worker who doesn't care about his performance is probably in the wrong job.

Maslow's hierarchy explains why simply paying higher wages is not an effective way to motivate personnel. When you reward an employee with a merit increase, it is for past performance. The individual is now able to satisfy his physiological needs on a higher level, but he does not relate past wage increases to his future performance on the job.

Frederick Herzberg, another psychologist, concluded from some research studies that there are two sets of factors that affect job satisfaction and performance: job content factors and what he called hygiene or maintenance factors. Job content factors had to do with growth, achievement, recognition, and advancement. These all had positive effects on job satisfaction when they were present but did not produce much dissatisfaction when they were absent. Hygiene or maintenance factors, which include wages, working conditions, supervision, status, security, company policy, administration, and other basic biological needs worked the opposite way. When these needs were not satisfactorily met, strong dissatisfaction resulted. When they were met, however, they did not contribute in any great degree to job satisfaction. From his findings, Herzberg developed the concept of job enrichment, that is, structuring each job to include opportunities for individual responsibility, achievement, recognition, growth, and advancement—the factors he identified as contributing to job satisfaction and therefore offering the greatest potential for motivation.

Motivation and Leadership

Let's relate Maslow's need hierarchy to motivational methods used by various styles of leadership described in the preceding chapter.

Autocrats

The authoritarian's primary method of motivation is fear of punishment. He demands obedience without question. The approach may be suited to short periods of stress and crisis when there is not time to go into all the details of the issue. In a restaurant during the heavy rush period, the supervisor says to the busboy, "Waterglasses!" That is a direct order to go and get glasses from the dishroom, an order issued in a stress situation. In times of stress, most people accept this type of leadership and even expect it, but it is far less acceptable under ordinary conditions. Then the primary response is to do only what is necessary to avoid punishment. There is no satisfaction of higher level needs. Since few people these days are forced to exist on the freedom from fear level, they find this situation unsatisfactory in a job situation, and they will look elsewhere for employment if they can.

Paternalist

The paternalist uses rewards, often in the form of parental approval, as his method of motivation. He has moved up one level on the hierarchy and appeals to the need for acceptance and love. For some people, especially those who are insecure, this can be an effective appeal.

The paternalist who can inspire confidence in his managerial and technical ability often becomes a teacher or mentor for young people just entering and learning the business. If the paternalist is not particularly able and successful, his subordinates will become impatient with his mediocre leadership and their inability to make their own contribution. The paternalist denies the capabilities of those under him and cuts them off from participation and from self development and advancement. When individuals are treated like children, they respond like children, operating on the fear-of-punishment level.

Democratic and Participative Leaders

Democratic and participative leaders generally have more success in motivating people because they appeal to higher level needs. They involve their staff in making decisions that will affect them. When the employee is involved in the management process, he becomes an important member of the team. The participative leader especially appeals to the self-actualization need on an individual basis.

Successful supervisors use a combination of leadership styles, depending on the situation and on the individuals involved.

Frustration and Typical Responses

What happens when needs are not satisfied? The answer is in one word—frustration. If this frustration is not released, the result is aggression. We have all heard the classic chain reaction.

1. The wife nags the boss at breakfast.
2. The boss yells at his men at work.
3. The man goes home and fights with his wife.
4. His wife hollers at the kids.
5. The kid goes out and kicks the dog.

How do people release frustration before it becomes aggression? One response is to escape, that is, leave the scene. This may take the form of quitting one's job or walking out.

Every dining room supervisor sooner or later has the experience of having a waiter or waitress walk out on his station in a stressful situation. The waiter is leaving the scene to avoid releasing his aggression in the wrong way. The other alternative may be to punch someone in the nose. Other types of escape are daydreaming and resignation. The resigned worker has ceased to care. He finds ways outside of his job to satisfy his belonging and self-actualization needs.

Another response to frustration is alternative behavior, that is, taking a detour to find some other way to satisfy a frustrated need. For example, if there is not enough silverware to go around, the staff will start to hoard it and take it from each other's stations in order to keep their tables set up. Another detour-type response is the grapevine. When management withholds information from the employees about matters that concern them, a grapevine develops. This informal information system feeds on rumors, tidbits, and misinformation.

The most satisfactory response to frustration is problem-solving behavior—that is, taking direct steps to resolve the conflict, remove the frustration, and satisfy a need. In the example above, problem-solving behavior would be a representative of the staff going to the boss to present their need for more silverware.

When these alternative responses to frustration are blocked, the aggression response is all that is left. Aggression may be physical violence against individuals or property, or it may be verbal violence and hostile behavior. If this type of behavior becomes evident to the guests in the dining room, it must be defused. Most individuals will attempt to inhibit such behavior publicly, but inhibited aggression becomes an even stronger force.

A person may release his aggression against himself instead of releasing it against others. He may drive his car recklessly and have an accident, develop headaches or ulcers, or try to drown his troubles in alcohol.

The supervisor is obviously not in a position to eliminate all causes of frustration in an employee's environment, but he must be prepared to deal with it when it affects staff performance.

When you are dealing with hostility and aggression, the immediate task is to defuse the situation, calm down the individual, and get his mind back on his work. Where more than one person is involved, get them apart and cool them off separately. It is vital that the supervisor keeps his cool. An angry boss only adds more fuel to the fire. Do not blame, condemn, or attempt to deal with the causes of the aggression as long as the participants are still hot.

Later on, take the time to sit down and calmly listen to the employee's side of the story and gather all the facts. The simple act of listening receptively without interruptions often relieves many pent-up frustrations and permits the person to examine his situation more rationally.

The first explanations given are usually not the real causes. At this point the supervisor must decide how deeply he wants to delve into factors that may be outside of the job situation. Very few supervisors are qualified to be guidance counselors and should not attempt to play that role. They can do more harm than good. If an employee needs help in dealing with personal problems, it is best to refer him to a professional counselor.

The supervisor's role should be to listen with understanding, without blaming or judging, without trying to impose or suggest a solution to the individual's problem. Allow the employee to sort out his thoughts and reach his own solution.

As for the job situation, work-related complaints should not be dismissed simply because "it was something else that was really eating him." These complaints most likely are real sources of frustration and should be investigated. If you are unreceptive to such complaints, you will turn off the flow of communication and future confidences. If an employee does not feel free to discuss a small complaint with his supervisor, he may bottle it up until it erupts as a big problem in the future. If the troops aren't doing a little griping now and then, something is wrong. It is the supervisor's job to find out what's bothering them and to resolve little problems before they become big ones.

A Customer-Oriented Attitude

In an earlier chapter we discussed the customer-oriented attitude. How do managers motivate their employees to care about their customers? All the handbooks and training classes in the world aren't going to change an individual's attitude toward people.

Developing a concerned, customer-oriented staff starts with the manager. If managers are not customer-oriented, the employees won't be either. But it goes beyond this. Managers must also care about the employees and treat them as mature, responsible members of the team. The way in which managers treat their employees quickly becomes the way in which the employees treat each other and the guests. It is the manager who creates the atmosphere in every restaurant. Whether he is open and supportive, small-minded and petty, or cold and self-centered, his way of interacting with people will filter through to the supervisors and the staff.

In a previous chapter we discussed human needs. Management must fulfill the employee's needs before the employee is able to meet the guest's needs. A waiter cannot be warm and gracious to the guest in the dining room when he has just been verbally attacked by the manager in the kitchen.

Finally, managers must require the customer-oriented attitude and performance 100 percent of the time. If you don't ask for it, you won't get it. Set the standard high, but be willing to bend a little once in a while. You may not get 100 percent performance all the time, but you will come much closer to it than you would have if you didn't ask at all.

Chapter 10

Controlling Dining Room Labor Cost

Payroll is by far the largest cost in the operation of a dining room. It includes not only the direct hourly wages of the service staff but also a number of related costs, sometimes referred to as "fringes." These include

1. The employer's share of social security taxes (At present this is 6.13 percent of each person's wages up to a maximum income of $25,900 for a total of $1,587.67.)
2. Federal and state unemployment insurance (Each employer's rate is based on the number of former employees drawing unemployment compensation.)
3. Workman's compensation insurance (This provides health care for employees injured on the job. The rate varies from state to state.)

These costs are set by law. In addition, most employers offer some type of paid vacation and sick pay. Many also pay all or part of the cost of health insurance and life insurance. If the staff is unionized, the union contract may require the employer to make contributions to union pension and welfare funds. Such contributions are usually figured on the basis of a set amount per union member or on the basis of manhours worked by union members each month.

Another group of costs directly related to the payroll are employee meals. Most employers provide free meals for their employees during their work shift. The cost of these meals is considered a part of the fringe benefit cost.

These related payroll costs can greatly increase the total payroll. In fact, in unionized companies, related payroll expenses can be as much as one-third of the total payroll or more.

These costs are considered part of total payroll, a cost for which the dining room supervisor is held accountable by management. There are other costs of employing people that are less easily identified but which exist none the less. Uniform cost is one. The cost of buying and laundering uniforms is usually not charged against specific departments, and it can be a considerable expense to a restaurant. If the company pays the service staff to maintain their own uniforms, this cost is easily identifiable by department.

Other hidden costs include preparing payroll each week, maintaining the extensive personal records required by the government, cleaning and maintaining employee locker rooms and lunchroom facilities, and performing various personnel functions—recruiting, training, and so forth.

Fortunately for the dining room manager, service payrolls are among the easiest to control in the restaurant. Most tipped employees prefer not to work if business is slow and their income from tips is down. The day to day mechanics of controlling labor costs include the following:

1. Scheduling based on forecasts of sales and standards of productivity
2. Controlling overtime
3. Providing proper information for preparing payroll and reviewing payroll reports

Before we can do effective scheduling, though, we must develop two essential management tools: productivity standards and staffing guides. Other, longer range tools (including job analysis and work simplification), the selection of productive employees, and a continuing program of training and retraining are also effective in controlling labor cost. Hiring and training are discussed in the following chapter. The final and perhaps most important factor in labor cost control is a motivated, productive staff that works together as a team. Motivation was discussed in Chap. 9.

Setting Productivity Standards

In large companies productivity standards or goals are often set by management. They may be expressed as covers served per manhour or in terms of sales dollars per manhour. If standards have not been established for your operation, you will have to establish your own standards. Since cover counts are easier to use, we will develop the standards on that basis rather than on sales; however, the principle is the same.

Separate standards must be established for each dining room and for each meal period based on the type of service used, the physical layout, the number of seat turnovers, and union contract terms. It is helpful to know what productivity you are now achieving. To get the overall rate, you need the total covers served during an average week and the number of hours worked by the service department for that week. The following formula is used:

$$\frac{\text{Total covers served}}{\text{Total hours worked}} = \text{Covers per manhour}$$

This computation provides a general measure of productivity. Now take it further and break it down by the various meal periods using the same basic formula.

$$\frac{\text{Total breakfast covers served}}{\text{Total hours worked for breakfast}} = \text{Covers per manhour for breakfast}$$

In making your analysis, use a test period of at least one week and choose a time when there are no unusual operating conditions that would distort the result, such as holidays or bad weather. Set up your results in a table like that shown in Fig. 10.1. (Figs. 10.1 through 10.8 will be used as examples throughout this discussion.) From this illustration you can quickly see which time periods have the lowest productivity and are pulling down your average. These periods should be examined first, although you will probably want to look at all segments of the operation to do a thorough analysis.

		AVERAGE COVERS	WAITER HOURS SCHEDULED	COVERS PER HOUR
BREAKFAST	6-11 AM	520	48	10.8
LUNCH	11-2 PM	450	36	12.5
AFTERNOON	2 -5 PM	175	12	14.6
DINNER	5-10 PM	435	46	9.5
LATE SUPPER	10-1 AM	125	12	10.4
TOTAL		1705	154	11.1

Fig. 10.1. Waiter productivity by meal period (for weekdays only).

For each meal period, go back and figure the productivity day by day and set those results in a table. Look at the days that had the highest productivity. On those particular days, was the staff pushed? Did service suffer? It isn't good to set standards at peak levels.

People can extend themselves for short periods of time when they have to but should not be expected to operate at that level all the time. Also, the object is not to cut back the level of service from our defined standards but rather to have sufficient staff on hand to provide that level at all times without overstaffing. Look also at the days with the lowest productivity levels. Were these times when you had the same amount of staff, but business was off? If you find that certain days of the week have particularly low productivity you have already identified areas for improvement in scheduling. You may also find some days with very high productivity caused by short staffing or an unusual influx of business. If you find any days with productivity too high to maintain or excessively low, eliminate them and take as your standard the average productivity of the remaining days. If weekend business patterns are different from weekdays, you may need to set a separate standard for them. Make this analysis for each meal period.

You have now established your first set of productivity or staffing standards. There is nothing mysterious about them. A standard is simply a measure that says how many manhours you should schedule for the number of meals you expect to serve. The same formula can be applied to the result to indicate how you actually did in comparison with the standard or goal. These first standards represent the average level you are presently achieving, with the low spots eliminated. Later we will discuss ways to increase productivity still further.

Developing Staffing Guides

The productivity standard is a tool for figuring out how many manhours the business will require for each meal period. The staffing guide shows how those hours should be scheduled in order to meet the demands of service without having unproductive labor. Staffing guides are shown in Figs. 10.2 and 10.3. Each person's hours are plotted by half

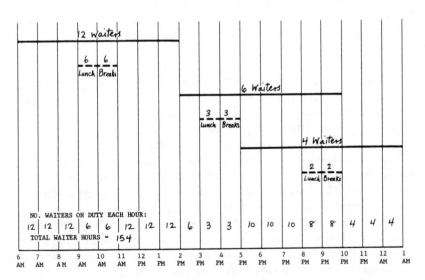

Fig. 10.2. Original staffing chart.

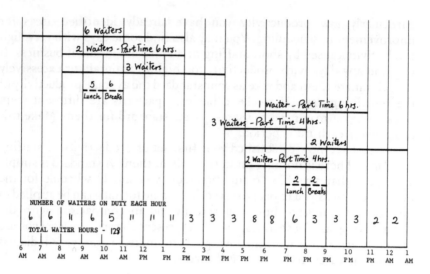

Fig. 10.3 Revised staffing chart.

hour, and the lunch breaks are also shown. The number of people on duty in each half-hour segment can then be quickly seen and compared to the flow of business in the same half-hour segment. When you add the amount of time required on each shift for setup and clean up, the staffing guide tells you when you have slack time and when your coverage is thin. Generally, a staffing guide is prepared for the median or average level of business. To provide flexibility for varying levels of business (since we budget our manhours on the basis of forecasts), the chart may show that certain shifts can be eliminated at low levels of business or added only for peak forecasts.

When the hours of staffing are plotted on a staffing guide, the result is usually a staggering of the shifts. This is what happened in the example. The entire staff was not needed for setup in the morning and is only present when the peak of business is reached. Since some come in later, they leave later and provide afternoon coverage. (The original staffing guide showed considerable slack time in the off-peak hours.) When waiters work in teams, staggered shifts are often a very effective scheduling method; one member of the team opens the station and the other closes. This provides continuity of service to the guest at the close of the meal period without holding waiters overtime.

Once you have plotted the shifts, you may find you can cut some slack time off the ends of the shifts and make a significant improvement in overall productivity without sacrificing the level of service during the actual serving period. If this is the case, you should go back and reevaluate your productivity standards in light of the revised staffing guides.

Forecasting the Business and Scheduling for the Week

Now you have the basic tools for staffing your dining room effectively. The first step in planning the weekly schedule is forecasting the amount of business that will be done each day for each meal period. In many restaurants, forecasts are regularly prepared by the manager; in others, they are made jointly by the dining room manager, chef, catering manager, and other department heads. If forecasts are not made in your operation, you must make your own. While it sounds difficult and impractical, forecasting skills can be developed with a little practice. First, you need to develop the sales history. If no records are kept of the number of covers served, you will have to start developing your own history. Your manager's logbook is a good tool if you enter the number of covers served at each meal as well as any events of the day that may have influenced the business, such as weather conditions, conventions in town, large parties, special local events (such as athletic events), and so forth. As you build this history, you will notice a pattern forming. Generally, two or three weeks' history is enough to start with, although a longer history is preferred. For holidays, of course, you would need to know what the pattern was last year.

Once you have some history, try to forecast the number of covers for the coming week. Check out the special events planned in the community, conventions, and so forth and use the past two or three weeks as a guideline. Then during the coming week, compare your estimate with the business you actually did. If you are within 5 percent of your forecast, you

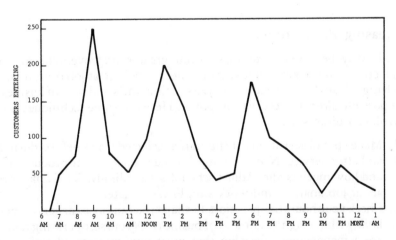

Fig. 10.4. Typical hourly flow of business: number of customers arriving each hour.

have done very well. There will be days when an unexpected event, such as a bad storm, will throw the count off. Since you don't staff a business for unexpected occurrences, it is best to label such a day in the history logbook as a fluke and discount it in future forecasts. Don't let such days prevent you from carrying on with your forecasts.

Scheduling: Computing the Hours

With forecasts for each meal period, you are ready to compute the number of waiter hours needed to service the forecasted business in the coming week. This is a simple calculation, dividing the total covers forecast for each meal period by the productivity goal for that period. If 300 covers are forecast for Monday lunch and the standard is 25 lunch covers per waiter, then 300/25 = 12 waiters required for Monday lunch. You can save time every week by setting up a little chart for yourself for the various levels of business you may experience for each meal period.

Lunch Staffing

Covers	Waiters
200	8
225	9
250	10
275	11
300	12

When you have the number of waiters required, all that remains is to identify the shifts on the manning chart that are to be filled for the day and assign the members of the staff to the various shifts.

Increasing Productivity

It may be possible to make even greater improvement in the productivity and reduce labor costs further by looking at job content and applying job analysis—that is, analyze starting times and flow of business and possibly alter the reservation policy. Here are some techniques that payroll consultants use.

1. Make spot observations of the staff at selected times before, during, and after service. Note how much time is really spent productively and how much is idle. Adjust schedules accordingly. We'll talk more about job analysis and work simplification later.
2. Check your hours of operation. Perhaps you can close earlier or open later without significant loss of business. Of course, operating hours are a management decision that must take into consideration all activities of the business, not only the dining room staffing.

3. Using the hourly flow of business (discussed in relation to the staffing guide), look at the troughs or slow periods to see where you could build sales volume by special promotions. Increasing sales does wonders for productivity and for the bottom line of the income statement.

4. If you have a reservations policy, review it in terms of your seating patterns and turnover. One luncheon club was able to get a partial second sitting, which is unheard of in that type of operation. They achieved it by using a no reservations policy. This forced members to come before 12:15 to be sure of getting a table, instead of 12:30 or 1:00, which is the usual time in this city. Members soon discovered that if they couldn't get to the dining room by 12:15, they could always get a seat around 1:30. As a result, the service hours were spread out and the number of covers a waiter could serve in a lunch period were increased. On the other hand, Windows on the World in New York is able to achieve two full turnovers a night by forcing reservations into two seatings. Reservations are accepted for seating between 5:00 and 6:30 and from 9:00 to 10:30. No reservations are accepted for the 6:30 to 9:00 period because the dining room is full during that time. A few walk-ins and late reservations may be sandwiched in if the first sitting vacates in time; otherwise, it's reservations only from 9:00 P.M. on.

Controlling Overtime

One area that can be very costly if not controlled is overtime. Companies that control labor costs carefully usually require some type of prior approval by management before overtime can be paid. Such policies must be well publicized to the staff. The employees must be aware that they cannot just set their own working hours and expect to be paid for them. Some favorite tactics are punching in an hour or two early, then taking an extra meal break or spending the time puttering about the dining room, setting up at a leisurely pace. At the end of the shift there are still guests on the station who must be served or sidework to be done, and suddenly overtime is necessary. Another trick is to delay and putter with closing duties, necessitating an extra hour or two to finish up. If these practices are allowed to continue, they suddenly become built in. There may be situations where overtime is unavoidable, as with banquets that break up later than scheduled. There may also be scheduling situations when an extra hour or two is really needed at the end of a shift. It may be less costly to pay the overtime premium than to bring in an extra person to cover. However, this is a decision the manager must make as part of his scheduling process, and must not be the prerogative of the employee.

Payroll Preparation

The last step in day-to-day labor cost control is proper preparation of payroll information. It is the responsibility of the dining room supervisor to see that the correct number of hours worked are reported to the payroll department. If meal breaks are not paid time, they must be subtracted from the hours worked. The company should also have a policy on docking for lateness. Finally, the supervisor should review the payroll after it is prepared to see that each person was paid for the correct amount of hours and at the proper rate. Employees are quick to tell you if they were underpaid but not so quick to report on overpayment.

Work Simplification and Job Analysis

Work simplification (the old time-and-motion study idea) is being used more and more in restaurants to improve productivity. While it is more applicable in kitchen and dishroom areas, it still may be a useful technique in improving the efficiency in some dining room functions.

Serving guests at tables is largely a matter of gathering items and carrying them either directly to the table or to a nearby service station. Some time may be saved by (1) shortening the distance to be traveled, (2) reducing the number of trips necessary (although your success in carrying out this suggestion will often depend on when the guests are ready for their next course), and (3) reducing the amount of time required to gather the items in the kitchen.

Industrial engineers use the technique of job analysis. First, they break down each task into its most basic components. These are usually classified according to the following categories:

1. Operation (for example, dip soup)
2. Inspection
3. Transportation
4. Delay or wait

Since transporting time and waiting add nothing to the value of the item, the objective is to reduce the time spent in these functions. For example, you can't eliminate a flight of stairs between the kitchen and the dining room, but you can cut down on the number of trips to the kitchen. Relocating coffee, rolls, salads, and desserts to a service pantry near the dining room would reduce the number of trips made to the kitchen. A communications system or electronic cash register point-of-sale computer terminal to transmit orders to the kitchen would eliminate other trips. Waits at the range for hot food would be eliminated by a signal device that would tell the waiter when his order is ready.

Storing equipment and supplies close to the point of use also reduces walking time. You may want to consider increasing the capacity of dining room side stands and organizing them to permit storage of all ware and supplies needed for a meal period. This would eliminate trips to the kitchen for refills during service. Often the space is there; it is only a matter of organizing it properly. Another time-and-motion technique is to store items that are used together in the same location. The beverage station should be set up with all the items needed for the service of beverages. If iced teaspoons are located next to the iced tea (along with ice, glasses, lemons, and underliners), the waiter will not have to make a separate trip to a side stand to pick them up.

Determine the quantities required for a day or a meal period and set up a standard supply schedule. Organize sidework and busboy duties so that these supplies get to the proper place before service. Avoid multiplication of the same function. Instead of having each captain send a waiter to the storeroom for the team's condiment and matches supplies, send one person for the entire department.

Another idea is to put things on wheels. Setup time can be reduced by wheeling dish dollies and glass racks into the dining room. One team sets the placemats and napkins for the entire room. A second team sets the silver, working off a cart that is rolled down the room. The third team sets the coffee cups and water glasses, working directly from the glass racks and dish dollies. This assembly line method cuts the setup time in half and is preferable to the old method in which each server has to make several trips to the kitchen, hunting down the equipment he needs and hand carrying it to his tables.

Another approach to work simplification involves asking the following questions about each task:

1. What is the task to be done?
2. Why is it really necessary?
3. When should it be done?
4. Who should do it?
5. How should it be done?

One supervisor asked, "Why is it necessary to vacuum the dining room carpet twice a day?" He purchased a carpet sweeper to use after lunch where needed and saved three-quarters of an hour. The carpet is vacuumed after lunch only if it is really needed.

In another restaurant, waitresses were spending too much time waiting for their toast to pop out of two small toasters. The supervisor requested installation of a larger rotary toaster. It was faster and had a larger capacity. When a waitress needed toast, she put two slices in and took the next two slices that came out. Although there was an occasional wasted slice, waiting time and stress were greatly reduced.

In an ice cream parlor, waitresses made their own sundaes and sodas. On a busy day this took a great deal of time away from their stations and caused considerable congestion and delay at the fountain. The supervisor assigned one person to be the soda jerk and was able to reduce the service staff by two waitresses, a net reduction of one person.

For many tasks, a single improvement made after applying work simplification techniques may not seem significant. However, when all of the various tasks are put together, there can be a visible improvement in the overall productivity of the department.

The Example Restaurant

Let's take another look at Figs. 10.1 through 10.8. These productivity charts are for The Example, a moderately priced 175-seat restaurant in a downtown area. It is open from 6:30 A.M. to 1:00 A.M. Monday through Saturday. The normal weekday staffing is as follows:

Early shift 6:00 A.M. to 2:00 P.M.: twelve waiters and waitresses
Middle shift 2:00 P.M. to 10:00 P.M.: six waiters and waitresses
Late shift 5:00 P.M. to 1:00 A.M.: four waiters and waitresses

Everyone gets a one-hour meal break and works a seven-hour day. This schedule requires 154 waiter-hours a day.

During a typical week, The Example serves 10,040 covers with an overall waiter productivity of 10.9 covers per waiter-hour. When Saturday activity is excluded, productivity is slightly higher (11.1). These figures indicate that Saturday productivity is lower than the average and is pulling down the overall waiter productivity. The largest volume of business is done during the week, however, and affords a greater potential for savings.

In Fig. 10.1 the Monday through Friday activity is broken down by meal period. Lunch time productivity is higher than the overall average, but dinner is below average. The highest productivity is achieved in the afternoon but on a very low volume of business.

The manager of The Example plotted the flow of business by hour (Fig. 10.4). This showed him where the business peaked. He also charted his staffing (Fig. 10.2) and computed the productivity hour-by-hour (Fig. 10.5). This showed him what he was achieving at peak periods and where the slack was in the schedule.

Now he began to develop his staffing standards by determining the coverage he needed to service the peak periods. There were at maximum twelve stations in the 175-seat dining room. The manager estimated that at lunch time people were seated, ate, and left in thirty minutes or less during the 12 noon to 1:00 P.M. period. Since parties of three are seated at tables for four and single guests are seated at deuces, it is unlikely that a waiter would have all of his seats occupied at any given time. Therefore, he assumed that only 75 to 80 percent of the chairs are occupied even when the restaurant is at full capacity. Thus the most a waiter could attain on a 16-seat station during the hour would be two sittings of 12 people or 24 covers. This figure represents an absolute maximum. It assumes that there is a waiting line and that whenever a table is vacated, another party is waiting to sit down. It also assumes that people are able to be served as quickly as they wish with no slowdowns or delays in service.

TIME PERIOD	COVERS	STAFFING-ORIGINAL	PRODUCTIVITY (COVERS PER WAITER HOUR)
6-7 AM	50	12	8.4
7-8	80	12	6.7
8-9	250	12	20.8
9-10	80	6	13.3
10-11	60	6	10.0
11-12	100	12	8.3
12-1 PM	200	12	16.7
1-2	150	12	12.5
2-3	75	6	12.5
3-4	40	3	13.3
4-5	60	3	20.0
5-6	175	10	17.5
6-7	100	10	10.0
7-8	80	10	8.0
8-9	60	8	7.5
9-10	20	8	2.5
10-11	60	4	15.0
11-12	40	4	10.0
12-1 PM	25	4	6.25
TOTAL OR AVERAGE	1705	154	11.1

*FOR FIRST HALF HOUR OF SERVICE

Fig. 10.5. Productivity by hour.

Using 24 covers per station or per waiter per hour, the manager estimated he could serve a maximum of 280 people in the peak lunch hour. In other words, for every 24 covers served in that hour, he needed one more waiter. This analysis shows that, for the week he studied, he only needed 8 waiters instead of 12 since he served an average of 200 people, not 280.

But there is a catch. With only eight waiters, he would have to either close down four stations, assign 22 seat stations, or do a combination of the two. Now what happens if the 200 guests do not arrive at even intervals and the dining room does not turn over according to plan? What would happen if three-quarters of them arrive at the beginning of the hour? If you are operating with reduced seating, you force 50 people to stand in line for a half hour, which would upset many guests on short lunch breaks. Or you could fill those big 22-seat stations and take the risk that some of the waiters will get stuck and give slow service. Between 8 and 12 waiters are needed for this situation. The manager decided to try it with 10.

Next, the manager examined the breakfast service. Here he assumed only a 60 percent utilization of seats since there are more single people and parties of two at breakfast than there are at lunch. He also used a maximum of 2.5 sittings per hour. This produced a maximum of approximately 260 people during the peak hour, very close to the 250 average during the week he analyzed (Fig. 10.4). With lower seat utilization, however, the manager felt the waiters could handle larger stations at breakfast than they could at lunch, and he decided to try working breakfast with 11 waiters instead of 12. Using the same method, he determined that dinner service required 8.

Finally, there are periods when a minimum staffing is required, regardless of the volume of business. For late supper, the manager wanted a minimum of two waiters on duty until closing. He also wanted at least three until 11:00 P.M. since the late supper business was somewhat unpredictable. By 11:00 P.M., however, they could usually tell what the rest of the evening's business would be like. If it looked like a rush, the third person could stay on another hour.

	AVERAGE COVERS	WAITER HOURS SCHEDULED	COVERS PER HOUR
BREAKFAST 6-11 AM	520	34	15.3
LUNCH 11-2 PM	450	33	13.6
AFTERNOON 2-5 PM	175	9	19.4
DINNER 5-10 PM	435	28	15.5
LATE SUPPER 10-1 AM	125	7	17.8
TOTAL	1705	111	15.4

Fig. 10.6. Waiter productivity with revised schedule (for weekdays only).

Now the manager had his peak hour requirements for breakfast, lunch, and dinner. Unfortunately, we cannot schedule workers only for the hour we need them; we must give them enough work to make it worth their while to come in. In fact, most union contracts require that a worker be paid for a minimum number of hours (usually four if he reports to work as scheduled. Therefore, the staffing required at peak times at least partially determines the staffing of off-peak periods. We can utilize off-peak times for meal breaks and side work, and we can employ part-timers for some of the time slots. Usually, though, it is difficult to find waiters to work only breakfast since tips are lower than at other meals. Most waiters want to work lunch as well to make their tips. Therefore, the manager at The Example had to revise his figures for lunch and schedule eleven waiters in order to have eleven for breakfast coverage. Now he charted his revised schedule and recalculated the productivity for each hour. In the periods where productivity was low, he tried staggering the shifts and substituting part-time help until he brought each time slot to an acceptable level. The final result is shown in Figs. 10.3, 10.6, and 10.7. He was able to cut the 6:00 A.M. opening crew from twelve to six by putting things on wheels to reduce setup time (see p. 81).

The revised schedule required 111 manhours as opposed to 154 required by the original schedule, a 28 percent reduction and an increase in productivity from 11.1 to 15.4. The largest increase was in late supper productivity, which rose from 10.4 to 17.8. This figure is a bit misleading,

TIME PERIOD	COVERS	STAFFING- ORIGINAL	PRODUCTIVITY (COVERS PER WAITER HOUR)	STAFFING- REVISED	PRODUCTIVITY
6-7 AM	40	12	6.6 *	6	13.3 *
7-8	90	12	7.5	6	15.0
8-9	250	12	20.8	11	22.7
9-10	80	6	13.3	6	13.3
10-11	60	6	10.0	5	12.0
11-12	100	12	8.3	11	9.1
12-1 PM	200	12	16.7	11	18.2
1-2	150	12	12.5	11	13.6
2-3	75	6	12.5	3	25.0
3-4	40	3	13.3	3	13.3
4-5	60	3	20.0	3	20.0
5-6	175	10	17.5	8	21.9
6-7	100	10	10.0	8	12.5
7-8	80	10	8.0	6	13.3
8-9	60	8	7.5	3	20.0
9-10	20	8	2.5	3	6.7
10-11	60	4	15.0	3	20.0
11-12	40	4	10.0	2	20.0
12-1 AM	25	4	6.25	2	12.5
TOTAL OR AVERAGE	1705	154	11.1	111	15.4
* FOR FIRST HALF HOUR OF SERVICE					

Fig. 10.7. Productivity by hour revised.

however, since the manager had provided himself with contingency coverage in case he needed it. The old schedule had been planned to cover higher levels of business even though they may not materialize. The new schedule provides flexibility. The gains in other periods were more concrete, however. Dinner increased from 9.5 to 15.5, a gain of 6 covers per man-hour. Breakfast showed a gain of 4.5 covers. These rates of productivity represent reasonable, attainable standards for the restaurant.

		MON	TUES	WED	THU	FRI	SAT
BREAKFAST	6:30AM-11AM	545	532	545	528	450	226
LUNCH	11-2 PM	436	427	445	463	479	483
AFTERNOON	2-5 PM	140	164	186	194	191	243
DINNER	5-10 PM	417	429	445	437	447	324
LATE SUPPER	10-1 AM	80	100	125	150	170	221
TOTAL		1618	1652	1746	1772	1737	1515

Fig. 10.8. Cover counts by day of the week.

We can take this analysis one step further. These productivity rates were established on the basis of an average. Averages are combinations of low values and high values. The covers served by day of the week are shown in Fig. 10.8. Generally, the counts are quite consistent. However, several are out of line. Friday breakfast, for example, is quite a bit lower than the rest of the week. If this is a regular occurrence, our standard reflects lower productivity for that meal period. On Monday business also seems to slacken after lunch. For late supper there is a wide range between the lowest day and the highest. Saturday, which we have not considered so far, shows a very different pattern of business. Separate standards could be set up for Saturday, using the same methodology the manager applied in developing his weekday schedule and standards.

Chapter 11

Training

Why train? Training is expensive. It ties up supervisors; takes workers away from their jobs; and requires space, training materials, and sometimes expensive equipment. After all this costly training, chances are the employee will quit anyway.

The answer is, of course, that while you have the employee, you have a trained employee, and trained employees are more productive than untrained ones. In the preceding chapters we discussed some of the factors related to job satisfaction and labor turnover. Individuals who are trained in their jobs are certainly more likely to derive satisfaction from doing their jobs well. They are also less likely to experience the frustration of job demands and situations they have not been prepared to cope with. For this reason, training itself works to reduce problems arising from high labor turnover.

Training should also be viewed as a long-term investment from which the company should get a return. There must be a measurable benefit from a training program, though this return may not be expressed in dollar savings. For example, one objective of a training program is to improve the quality of work performed and raise it to the established standards. This should reduce customer complaints and increase the volume of business. As employees become more proficient in their jobs, productivity and morale improve and staff turnover is reduced. The overall effect is reduced labor costs. With proper training, employees in lower-echelon jobs can be upgraded to more skilled positions as the need arises. A policy of advancement from within also contributes to a high level of staff morale. In addition, training reduces waste, breakage, and accidents.

Training Programs in Restaurants

The Sink-or-Swim Method

This method is nontraining. It assumes a new employee is an experienced worker and can walk right into the job and start work. The employee may be experienced but not in *this* restaurant and not serving *this* menu.

The sink-or-swim method, which is still used in some restaurants, obviously does not provide the new employee with the information he needs to do his job properly. What is worse, it says something about the attitude of management toward employees. It tells the new employee that he is not important; management cannot be bothered with him. As we have seen in the previous chapter, this is not the way to motivate an individual on the job. Total negligence of the training responsibility is a major cause of high labor turnover.

The Buddy System

In the buddy system the new employee is assigned to follow an experienced employee for a few days before he is given a station of his own. During that time, the experienced worker is supposed to train him. This system relieves management of the job of training and places it on an employee. Some employees may consider it a compliment to be a trainer, but others may consider it a burden, especially if it cuts down on their tips. The real problem with this method is that few workers are good trainers. It is even harder when they are trying to perform their own jobs at the same time. Few people can do two jobs at once and do both well. Something has to suffer—usually, the trainee.

There is another disadvantage to this system of training. Waiters and waitresses as a group are quite mobile, moving frequently from job to job and from town to town. Through their different work experiences, they develop a set of work habits and ways of serving that may or may not be acceptable to their current employer. Any bad habits they bring to their present job are usually passed on to new employees they train. Because of this, some operators prefer to hire completely inexperienced people and train them in their own style of service, thus creating a need for some type of formalized training program. Since there are always new employees entering the organization, this training must be ongoing.

JIT—Job Instruction Training

JIT was originally developed to quickly train unskilled defense workers during the Second World War. The JIT motto was, "If the worker hasn't learned, the instructor hasn't taught!" It is still used as the basis for training programs in most industries. JIT breaks down instruction into four steps: (1) prepare the worker, (2) present the operation, (3) try out performance, and (4) follow up.

1. Prepare the worker. Put him at ease and find out what he already knows about the job. Get him interested in learning the job.
2. Present the operation. Tell, show, illustrate, and question carefully and patiently. Stress key points. Instruct clearly and completely, taking up one point at a time.
3. Try out performance. Test him by having him perform the job. Have him tell and show you; have him explain key points. Ask questions and correct errors. Continue until *you* know he knows.
4. Follow up. Put him on his own. Designate someone he can go to for help. Check frequently. Encourage questions. Get him to look for key points as he progresses. Allow the coaching and close follow up to taper off.

Before teaching, the instructor must prepare. JIT lists four steps.

1. Set a timetable. How much do you expect him to learn and how soon?
2. Break down the job. List principal steps. Pick out key points.
3. Have everything ready—the proper equipment, materials, and supplies.
4. Arrange the work place just as you expect the worker to keep it.

Total Training Program

JIT deals with teaching a specific operation or task. The new restaurant employee needs to learn an entire series of tasks and more. Here is where the total training program comes in. It provides the new employee with an introduction to the company (its benefits and regulations), an introduction to his job, and shows him where he fits into the total organization. The program demonstrates to the new employee that his job is important and that he is important to the company. This is the first step in retaining the employee and reducing labor turnover.

Next, the new employee is introduced to his particular assignment, his supervisor, and coworkers. The program then moves the new employee into task instruction, which leads to actual supervised work performance.

The total training program continues to monitor the employee's performance as he gains experience, to identify areas of substandard performance, to provide periodic refreshers, and to keep experienced employees current on new techniques and information.

Requirements of a Successful Training Program

To be successful, a training program must have a specific objective. Without it, the trainers will be operating in a vacuum. We have already mentioned some typical training program objectives.

- To improve the quality of service and raise it to the established standards
- To reduce customer complaints
- To increase productivity and reduce labor cost
- To reduce waste
- To reduce accidents

These objectives are closely related to the basic goals of the company. In fact, training specialists state that without the support of top management, no training program can be successful. Training must be supported at all levels of the organization, from the top management who authorize the investment to the line supervisors who carry out the program. Without ongoing training, the survival and growth of the enterprise is in jeopardy.

Another requirement of a successful training program is a motivated trainee. No training can be successful if the employee does not want to learn. He will be motivated, however, if he believes he will benefit in a direct way. Of course, new employees want to learn so that they will be able to perform the job properly.

A program introduced at an established operation may meet resistance from long-timers. These employees may perceive the program as something new and strange, representing a radical change from the way they have been doing things. They may also feel insulted, that their years of experience are being ignored and that they are being classed as rank beginners. Either way, a new training program is seen as a threat. Management must present a training program as having a direct benefit for both experienced and new employees. Better service means more business and larger tips.

A successful training program also needs supervisors who know how to train. It may mean that the first step in implementing the program is to train the trainers.

Finally, the program needs a detailed plan and a time schedule. It should not be allowed to ramble along with training sessions scheduled when time is available. In addition, there should be follow up to insure that the objectives of the program are met.

Training Methods

A training program may use a combination of methods: classroom instruction, reading materials, one-to-one instruction by the supervisor, or self-instruction (which may include the use of sophisticated audiovisual materials). Whatever the method, each new employee should have a defined program and a time schedule to accomplish the program.

When large numbers of employees are hired, initial introduction into the company is done in groups, meeting in classroom-type situations, usually with a training specialist from the personnel department. This type of training is usually information-giving. The employee learns about the company—its benefits, policies, work rules, and general personnel procedures. These sessions are then followed with an introduction to the employee's supervisor, a tour of the premises, and introductions to other personnel with whom he will be working.

Usually, however, there are only one or two new employees at a time. The information-giving type of training must then be handled on an individual basis. This is usually done with a booklet and, in a large company, may be supplemented with a short video film welcoming the person. The personal contact must be supplied by the supervisor instead of a training specialist. It is important that this contact be friendly and welcoming and that the individual is made to feel that he belongs to the organization.

The new employee then begins a period of training in the specific skills of his new role or job. This type of training is instructional in nature. Few companies are large enough to warrant classroom-type training for each of the different job skills required in a restaurant. Training is done on an individual basis, usually by the department supervisors. Ideally, some combination of self-instruction and supervised instruction is used to permit the supervisor to perform his many other functions.

Materials used for teaching skills are usually very structured. Following the JIT program, each task is presented separately. In a waiter training program, for example, a task may be one of the steps of service, a sidework assignment, or a service detail for a particular menu item. The task may be presented in written form, illustrated with pictures and diagrams. Key points are stressed, and the trainee may be asked to respond to questions in a workbook. If he does not answer the questions correctly, he can go back and review. The written material may be supplemented with short videotape demonstrations. Later the trainee may observe the performance of the task in actual service by trailing an experienced, trained waiter. After the meal service, the supervisor may ask the trainee to try out the task by serving him. It is important that this tryout be done in a safe situation where the trainee is free to make a mistake and can be corrected by the supervisor. As the trainee progresses, he studies more tasks until he is finally permitted to work regular service. He may be assigned to serve one table at first, with the supervisor close by. As he gains speed and proficiency, the trainee's station size is increased and the amount of direct supervision is reduced.

Even when he has had experience elsewhere, the new employee should still receive the same training program as the beginner. However, he should be permitted to proceed through the task instructional material at his own pace. He may only need a review of the menu items and details of service steps since he will be able to relate this new information to his past experiences. He should still have a tryout and observation period, during which the supervisor should be alert to any bad habits the new employee has carried over from previous jobs.

However, training should not end here. It is an ongoing function requiring reinforcement of past training and retraining for new menu items, new policies, and new procedures.

The daily lineup is a training tool. It provides a few minutes each day to refresh a technique or to correct a service that may have slipped. It is also a time to briefly present new material. Generally, the lineup is better suited to information-giving, rather than instruction.

When there is a major change in procedure, such as the introduction of a new menu, longer sessions are required. These may be held classroom-style before or after the meal service. Here again, the nature of the training is usually to give information rather than instruct. Experienced personnel will be able to apply their past instructional training to the new information presented. For example, a class to familiarize the staff with new wines on the wine list will be mostly informational in nature since the personnel presumably already know how to serve wines.

Training Materials

There are a number of very good training materials and films available. (The National Restaurant Association has an excellent catalog listing not only training films and manuals but also books and pamphlets on all aspects of food service management. Their address is One IBM Plaza, Suite 2600, Chicago, Illinois, 60611.) These materials provide general instruction in table service, though they may not be suited to a particular operation. A theme or specialty restaurant may need to develop some customized supplementary materials. Videotape has proven to be an effective medium. It is easy to make, efficient to use, and relatively inexpensive. This last item is an important consideration when materials must be updated periodically for new menu items.

Appendix C contains a selection from a training manual for The Corner, a restaurant in New York City's World Trade Center. The manual contains general instructions concerning appearance and conduct on the job as well as a sample task description.

Other Sources of Training

A number of communities have courses available to meet special needs. While it may be too costly to send an entire staff for training, specialized courses, such as a wine course or a class on supervision or merchandising, may supplement in-house training programs for specialized jobs.

In larger cities, some trade unions offer a selection of classes for their members. The National Restaurant Association and some of the state restaurant associations have seminars from time to time. Local trade schools, colleges, and correspondence schools may also have courses of interest. Wherever possible, such programs may supplement those offered in-house.

Hiring New Employees—Recruiting Sources

Let's back up a moment. We said that one of the requirements of a successful training program was a motivated trainee. Where do you find motivated trainees? The hiring process is a critical step in the development of an effective, productive staff.

The sources used to recruit new employees will vary depending on the local labor market and the type of employee sought. Typical sources are:

- Advertisements in newspapers
- Advertisements in specialized media, such as local restaurant journals and newsletters
- Private agencies
- Government agencies
- Student placement services at schools
- Referrals from present employees
- Union hiring halls
- Walk-ins

There are advantages and disadvantages to each of these sources. Advertisements in daily or weekly newspapers reach a wide readership at relatively low cost. The disadvantage is that they often produce a large number of applicants, many of whom will not be suited for the job. Unless the company has a personnel officer who can do prescreening, managers and supervisors may have to spend considerable time interviewing and screening candidates.

Private agencies require a fee, which can be quite high. They do perform a screening function, however. Because of the economics involved, agencies are not a usual source of hourly personnel but may be used to hire skilled or supervisory-level candidates.

Government agencies do not charge a fee, but the caliber of applicants supplied by state agencies is usually not very high. Student placement offices in schools and colleges may be a very good source for recruiting certain positions. There is usually no fee involved. The difficulty with student labor is that it tends to be seasonal; that is, students want to work during the school year and take time off for exams and vacations.

Many employers say their best source for recruitment is their own employees. In fact, for most positions it may be their only source. The applicant has already been prescreened by the referring employee. There is no cost involved, and there is a high probability that the new person will work out because the referring employee has an interest in seeing that he does.

Unions

In some unionized companies, jobs must be posted with the unions. However, there is no requirement that a union candidate be hired. For operations that prefer to hire experienced and trained waiters, the union is a good source. The problem is that at any given time, the pool of waiters looking for jobs usually contains a high proportion of poorer workers; the better ones are already employed.

Walk-ins

Occasionally a job applicant will walk in off the street on the chance that the restaurant may be hiring. Walk-ins are usually seeking unskilled jobs. Generally, most managers consider walk-ins a poor source for desirable workers.

Hiring Procedures

All candidates should be required to complete an application for employment. This need not be a complicated form but should include certain pertinent information: name and address, telephone number, social security number, past employment history, education, and references.

The candidate should then be interviewed to determine his general suitability for employment. This preliminary interview may be conducted by someone other than the supervisor or manager. In larger companies it is done by the personnel office. The preliminary interview should establish evidence of the candidate's stability, as indicated by length of time at present address and length of time in previous job, and a reasonable reason for leaving his previous employer. The interviewer should also establish the type of work the candidate is seeking, the salary range, and the working hours. He should review the information on the application blank for legibility, completeness, and accuracy. He should look for evidence that the applicant is able to work with other people and take direction and that he appears to have a state of health adequate for the job. If the candidate meets these preliminary requirements and the job opening is what he is seeking, he is then scheduled for a second interview with the department supervisor. In this second interview, the supervisor examines the candidate's qualifications for the specific job opening.

Typical job requirements for service personnel are a clean, neat, and pleasant appearance; an alert, courteous attitude; a calm temperament and even disposition; and the ability to read and speak English and do simple arithmetic computations. The candidate must be able to stand for long periods of time and to carry heavy trays. In operations serving alcoholic beverages, the applicant must meet minimum standards required by state liquor laws.

In addition, the supervisor will ask the applicant about his previous work experience to establish the type of jobs held previously, reasons for leaving, and what the applicant liked and disliked about his previous positions. Answers to this type of question can indicate how the person will adapt to the new work situation.

If the candidate meets the job qualifications, he may be hired pending a reference check and a physical examination. References should be checked regardless of how promising the applicant may appear. The check should include the applicant's last employer, but only if the applicant is no longer working for him. A current employer should be contacted only if the applicant gives his consent.

Personnel officers usually prefer to make reference checks by telephone. The information can be obtained quickly and follow up questions can be asked. Another advantage to the telephone check is that people will say things on the phone that they would not put in writing. Their tone of voice can also provide clues, which can be followed up with further questions.

Hiring Standards and the Law

Title VII of the Civil Rights Act of 1964 and the Equal Employment Opportunity Act of 1972 prohibit discrimination of job applicants. These statutes make it unlawful for an employer to "fail or refuse to hire or to discharge any individual or otherwise discriminate against any individual" on the basis of race, color, religion, sex, or national origin. Another federal law, the Age Discrimination in Employment Act, prohibits discrimination against persons 40 to 65 years old.

These laws have considerable implications for hiring in restaurants. The Equal Employment Opportunity Commission (EEOC), which administers these laws, takes a very narrow view of what constitutes a "bona fide occupational qualification." This means that any requirement that may bar employment to members of a discriminated class (for example, blacks or women) must be proven to be "necessary to the normal operation" of the business. Thus a claim by a luxury restaurant that "female waiters would not be accepted by the guests" is not a valid defense in support of a job requirement that the service staff be male. In a continental restaurant, however, requiring captains to speak fluent French and to have a good working knowledge of French wines and cuisine would be considered a bona fide occupational qualification. Even when a skilled requirement is valid, an employer may still be guilty of discrimination if prevailing conditions were such that a discriminated class was prevented from acquiring the necessary skills for reasons of race, sex, color, religion, or national origin. The employer may be required to provide training to members of a discriminated class and to meet predetermined quotas for the skilled jobs in future hiring.

In 1977 a suit was brought against a group of luxury restaurants in New York City to require them to employ women as waitresses and captains. The suit claimed that sex was not a bona fide occupational qualification. Some of the restaurants named in the suit settled by agreeing to employ a certain percentage of females in these positions within a prescribed time. A number of the restaurants claimed, however, that there were an insufficient number of women qualified for the positions. Several volunteered to provide training for any serious applicant.

The Privacy Act of 1974 prevents employers from asking prospective employees certain questions, such as those concerning arrest records or medical conditions. Other areas of questioning that may be seen as discriminatory are also prohibited. These include credit reference checks, marital status, method of birth control, or plans to have children (asked of women only). An interviewer must be prepared to show why his line of inquiry does not discriminate against the prospective employee.

Chapter 12

Supervising a Unionized Staff

Unions are a fact of life. They are here to stay, and we must live with them. The fact of unions is neither good nor bad. Some unions are better managed than others. Some are more effective than others in protecting the rights of their members. However, no union can take away management's right to manage *unless management itself has bargained away that right.* This is an important point. The practices that union contracts cover have to deal with certain basic points: economic issues such as wages and fringe benefits, job security, grievances, and union security. Working conditions and rules may also be covered. All of these are mechanisms to protect the worker from arbitrary and unfair management practices. In fact, union leaders have acknowledged that management invites unionization through poor management practices. Where employees are reasonably paid and secure in their positions, unions have great difficulty in gaining a foothold.

The Supervisor's Role in Unionized Companies

The supervisor is the first line of management. It is his job to carry out the terms of the contract, a contract which he probably did not participate in making. It goes without saying that the supervisor must know the terms of the contract to the letter. Not only must he know what the contract does say, he must know what it *doesn't* say. Anything not expressly prohibited by the contract is permitted (unless prohibited by law or other authority, such as company regulations or policy). Some managements, however, are fearful of taking any action they feel the union might object to. This attitude can severely limit the supervisor in carrying out his responsibilities and can create precedents that may be very damaging in future negotiations.

Just as the supervisor represents management, the union steward represents the union membership—the employees. It is his job to see that the terms of the contract are carried out. Some stewards, especially newly elected ones, can be a pain in the neck, nit-picking about every minor incident, real or imagined. Others can be highly effective in maintaining the morale and enforcing the work rules in the company. The relationship between shop steward and supervisor usually is a matter of individual personalities and the amount of effort each puts forth in building a good working relationship. Even in companies where labor-management relations have a history of bad blood, individuals can establish a good relationship if they feel it is in their best interest to do so.

The supervisor can improve his side of the relationship by recognizing that it is the steward's job to see that the contract is enforced by the members. Of course, in every contract there are areas of interpretation. The steward is entitled to his interpretation, and the supervisor is entitled to his. The supervisor should also remember, though, that supervisors are not infallible, and he should expect the steward to point out his mistakes.

On the other hand, the supervisor should expect the steward to recognize that managing the department is the supervisor's job, and employees are expected to follow his directives. If they disagree with an order, they are still obligated to carry it out. Later they can file a grievance if they wish.

Both the supervisor and the shop steward are working for the same basic goal—that is, long-term profits. Without profits, neither the company nor the employees' jobs will survive.

The Union Contract

The parts of the contract that most concern the supervisor are those dealing with hiring terms, scheduling, job classification, and grievance procedures.

Grievances

The contract will probably spell out the steps to be taken in handling a grievance. Generally, it is in the best interest of the company to settle grievances between employee and supervisor on the spot and without delay. The supervisor must handle each case on its own merit based on the facts, not on emotional interpretations, assumptions, or hearsay. Whether the resolution satisfied the employee or not, the complaint and its disposition should be written up in detail in the department log with all relevant facts included. This provides management with information on the matter in case it surfaces again. It also contributes to a history that can be very useful in identifying sources of complaints and possible need for contract revision in future negotiations.

If the supervisor's decision is not satisfactory to the employee, he has the right to take his grievance to higher management. At this point, the union steward usually becomes involved. After hearing the employee's side, the steward may advise him that he has no case, and the matter is closed. If the steward feels the employee has a case, the formal grievance procedure is initiated; the grievance is put in writing and submitted to the next level of management. If the matter reaches the highest level in the company without being satisfactorily resolved, the contract may state that it must go to an impartial arbitrator whose ruling is binding. Since arbitration is costly, the expense is usually shared by the union and the company. Depending on whether or not the company may be affected in the future by precedents set in arbitration, the company will decide whether or not it wants to fight the grievance. If little is at stake, it may rule at a lower level in favor of an employee, reversing the ruling of the first-line supervisor in order to keep the peace. Supervisors should be aware that this may be the outcome of a grievance, and if they are in doubt about making their charges stick, they should check with their superiors first.

Working Hours, Meal Breaks, and Length of Workday

Another part of the contract will deal with such factors as length of workday, premiums for overtime, meal breaks, and allowances for changing of uniforms. It may also specify conditions for days off on weekends and weekdays.

These terms must be considered when scheduling and also when preparing information for payroll. A supervisor may find, however, that the company has inadvertently been paying for things that are not really required by the contract. If the practice has been of short duration, the company stands a good chance of getting it corrected. If the practice has been going on for a long time, the union may consider it a past practice that must be continued even though it is not specified in the contract. Arbitrators have upheld this position in previous cases. If you find a situation like this, you should bring the matter to management's attention before attempting to do anything about it. In the future, beware of setting a precedent that could become a bothersome past practice in the future.

Hiring Terms

A contract may provide for the hiring of new employees on a provisional basis for a certain period of time. During this time, the employment may be terminated for any reason. After the provisional period, the employee may be terminated only for cause. If you do not take action quickly to dismiss a provisional employee whose performance is not satisfactory, you may be stuck with him.

Job Classifications and Descriptions

Most contracts contain a list of job titles and their negotiated wage rates without a detailed description of each job. In table service restaurants, job content is defined by tradition. For an existing restaurant, the job consists of whatever the individual was doing in that job in the past. However, there are gray areas. In one restaurant, it is the busboy's job to vacuum the dining room carpet; in another restaurant, this job is done by a porter. Waitresses in a coffee shop usually draw their own beer; in a table service restaurant, a bartender may draw it for them. In one private club, a captain relieves on the maître d's day off; in another, the manager performs this job. In one restaurant, waiters bus their own tables if they have time and the busboy is busy. In the establishment down the street, waiters wouldn't think of bussing a table. These are some of the gray areas that exist when there are no defined job descriptions.

It is difficult to state generalities in realigning job content; but as a rule, the union is most concerned about maintaining the relative distinctions between skill levels for the jobs and their related wage scales. In the case of vacuuming, there is not much difference between the busboy level and the porter job, except that the busboy is usually considered a tipped employee. If the busboy would receive less in tips as a result of his taking on vacuuming duties, the union could require that he be paid a higher rate for vacuuming time. In the case of waiters bussing tables, the situation is not as clear. If it could be shown that the waiters would serve more customers and therefore increase their income if they bussed tables, they would probably accept such a change in job content. However, if this change meant that the waiter staff would be cut (and therefore produce less revenue for the union in dues and welfare contributions), the union might object.

Skill level is another consideration. Asking higher paid employees to perform lower rated jobs, such as asking a waiter or captain to vacuum, would probably produce opposition. In a young, recently opened restaurant, there are no precedents, and management has more freedom in determining job content (unless the new restaurant is one of a chain, in which case precedents have been established in other units). The last defense against rigid job content is having written job descriptions that are general enough to permit flexibility when needed, but still provide a workable description of the job.

In restaurants that are innovative or offer new concepts, there is also less opposition to nonconventional job contents. The more progressive unions are recognizing the need to increase productivity in order to save existing jobs and create new ones. Combination jobs, such as having a bartender serve a limited number of food items at the bar, is a recent development. Under less enlightened conditions, a restaurant wishing to have hot, carved sandwiches at a stand-up bar would have been required to staff the operation with a bartender and a carver, regardless of the volume of business.

Where job content is long established, making changes is difficult, even with union cooperation. It is best to make a number of very small changes to avoid a major upheaval in the operation. It is not easy to change habits and practices that have been in effect for years. Even the smallest change in routine can be very upsetting to some people, especially older employees. The best advice is to move slowly. Sooner or later you will accomplish your goals.

The Supervisor's Role in Contract Negotiation

In all probability, you will not be asked to participate in contract negotiations. They are usually handled by top management and labor lawyers. You can, however, play a part in negotiations by making recommendations ahead of time concerning contract terms that are especially bothersome. Some companies have formal planning sessions with supervisors prior to negotiations to solicit this type of information and to get their opinions on contract clauses under consideration. Your department logbook is especially useful in providing specific cases and details.

Union Organizing Drives

If your company is engaged in a union organizing drive, you should be instructed by management as to what you may or may not do. Federal regulations are very explicit about what constitutes an unfair labor practice. You should be very familiar with these regulations so you will not accidentally cause the company to be in violation of the law or jeopardize the company's bargaining position.

Generally, during a union organizing drive, you should do the following:

1. If a union representative approaches you, refer him to the manager in a courteous manner. Do not engage in any conversation or discussion with him. If he approaches employees during working hours or on company property, inform the manager at once. You do not have to permit him access to nonpublic areas of the restaurant.

2. Do not discuss the union drive with the employees. Management will probably state the company's position to all employees at one time. You may jeopardize the company's position by making illegal statements.

3. Do not single out antiunion employees for special favors or prounion employees for disciplinary action, such as dismissal or layoff.

Chapter 13

Cashiering
and Revenue Control

There are two ways of collecting cash in table service restaurants. The customer either makes his payment directly to a cashier, or he pays the waiter (who then settles with the cashier). A variation of this second method is to have the waiter maintain his own bank and settle with the cashier (or manager) once at the end of the shift. This procedure is used in some counter service operations where each counter has its own cash register, and in some cocktail lounges and restaurants as well.

In large restaurants, the dining room supervisor is not usually responsible for cashiering. In small operations, especially fast turnover restaurants where the customer pays the cashier directly, the supervisor may be responsible for the cashiering function.

Whatever system is used, whether or not the dining room supervisor is responsible for the actual collection of the revenue, he *is* responsible for seeing that his staff charges correctly for the items they serve, that all money collected is turned in to the cashier, that customers are not overcharged or otherwise cheated, and that customers do not walk out without paying.

Common Control Systems in Table Service Restaurants

In the old hotel system, checkers were stationed in the kitchen. Guests' orders were written down on an order pad. This order was then taken to the checker who assigned a guest check to the waiter and wrote out the order again on his hard check. The checker then entered the prices on the check either by hand or by machine. When the waiter assembled his order, he took it to the cashier station. There, the checker lifted all the lids and inspected the tray to be sure all items were listed on the check.

When the guest was ready to settle the check, the checker totaled it and prepared a detailed record of the check and the charges. The waiter then collected cash from the guest (or had the check signed for a charge) and turned in the check and cash collected to a cashier who completed the transaction. At the end of the meal, the cashier's records had to match the checker's records. If a check was missing, the waiter was held responsible for the amount as recorded by the checker.

The rising cost of labor has made the checker system practically obsolete. Checking is more often done on a test basis by managers, captains, or controller's representatives. The precheck system is most often used. Here, the waiter is assigned a number of guest checks. When he takes an order, he records the items on the check. He then takes it to a precheck machine where he enters the prices and totals. This priced check is presented to the barman or chef to obtain food or drinks. These individuals will not give out any food or beverage that has not been rung up on the check. A variation of this system uses a machine with a throwcheck or ticket that is turned in instead of the check. Some checks have duplicate copies or stubs that are submitted in place of the check itself.

When the guest pays, the waiter takes the check and cash (or charge) payment to a cashier station where the transaction is rung up on a cash register. The cashier rings the amounts for food, beverages, tax, and other charges on the back of the check.

At the end of the day, the amounts entered on the precheck machine should match the amount of cash and charges collected, as shown on the cashier's register.

The key points in these control systems are as follows:

1. Control of guest checks. Waiters cannot present a check to a guest for payment and then pocket the money and destroy the check. All checks must be numbered consecutively and be accounted for (including reserve stocks).
2. Control of merchandise issues. Main entrée and drink charges must be entered on the guest check before the waiter can pick up the items. This control is not usually extended to appetizers, desserts, and other lesser valued items, although it may be if necessary.
3. Comparison of merchandise issued from the kitchen (according to the chef's records) with the sales recorded on guests' checks. Electronic point-of-sale equipment makes this type of control very simple by tabulating sales in numbers of portions of each item as well as in dollars. Without this type of equipment, tabulation must be done manually.
4. Comparison of guest check totals with detail tapes in registers. This would be done on a test basis only, or if a discrepancy were found.

5. Comparison of the dining room manager's cover count with the total number of covers on guest checks.

In fast service restaurants with low average checks, the cost of an elaborate prechecking system is usually not warranted. An additional consideration is speed. Such an operation depends on fast turnover of seats to offset low checks. Therefore, any control system used should not slow down service. In this type of operation, controls still require accounting for checks and may include comparison of kitchen production against sales on checks. Other aspects of control usually require direct, on-the-spot supervision. Waiters should be required to price out their checks and leave them on the table or counter when the main course is served. Room supervisors can look to see that checks are properly made out and include all items that have been served to that table.

Cashiering Procedures

Cashiers must be impressed with the importance of following proper procedures in handling money and the need for arithmetic accuracy in preparing their reports. They should be required to sign a statement to the effect that any funds assigned to them are the property of the company and that they will bear full responsibility for all overages and shortages. State labor laws vary on the employer's right to make employees pay the amount of a shortage. But even if the employee cannot be forced to pay, such a statement still has psychological value. In addition, all employees who handle cash should be bonded.

Cashiering procedures should be written out in detail and available at every cashier station. New employees should be thoroughly trained in these procedures and required to follow them at all times. Listed below are some general procedures that may be used as guidelines. Detailed procedures will vary, depending on the type of operation and the register equipment used.

1. Prior to opening for business, the cashier should count the bank to confirm that the correct amount of money is there. As a rule, a cashier's bank is maintained at the same amount, and the cashier is required to sign for this amount when it is initially issued. If the amount of the bank is changed, the cashier should be required to sign a new receipt showing the amount of the revised bank.
2. The cashier station should be kept orderly at all times. All bills and coins should be put into the correct sections of the cash drawer.
3. When a customer presents a check and money for payment, the cashier should verbally acknowledge the amount of the check and the amount of money rendered. He should examine the bills carefully, especially those of large denomination and comment if

there are any unusual markings on a bill. It may be a setup for a short change artist, or the bills may be counterfeit. Any unusual transaction should be referred to the manager or supervisor.

4. The cashier then places the bill on the cash register slab. He inserts the check into the register slot and rings up the amount of the sale according to the instructions for his type of register. If both cash and charge sales are handled, the register will have separate keys for the two types of transactions. Electronic equipment may have a separate key for each type of credit card accepted. It may also compute the amount of change to be returned.

5. The cashier should always count the change twice, once as he removes it from the register and once as he hands it to the customer. If the register does not compute the amount of change to be given, the cashier should start with the amount of the check and then count up to the amount of cash rendered.

6. When the transaction is completed, the customer's bill is then placed in the proper section in the register and the drawer is closed. The guest check is removed from the register slot and put in a check box or rack (usually with separate slots for each waiter).

7. Under no circumstances should the cashier leave his station without locking the register. Furthermore, he should keep the drawer shut when not putting money in or taking it out. If a coin falls on the floor, he should give the customer another coin from the cash drawer and look for the lost coin later.

8. The cashier should look at each customer directly when handling the transaction. Eye contact can put off a potential thief because he may think the cashier suspects his intent and is memorizing his appearance.

9. The cashier should complete one transaction at a time and not permit customers or others to interrupt. A typical tactic of the short change artist is to confuse a cashier by requesting several types of transactions at the same time.

10. In the event of an error or misring on the register, the total amount of the ring should be recorded on a cashier's correction sheet. The entire transaction is then rung again—this time, correctly. Cashiers should not try to deduct or adjust on a subsequent transaction. Splitting rings or bunching should also be discouraged. Each transaction should be rung separately and correctly, just as it appears on the guest check. Completed checks should then be register validated.

11. Making payments out of the cash drawer is a practice auditors and tax agents frown upon. The only paid-outs that are considered legitimate are payments to service staff for tips charged on credit

cards or house accounts. These payments should be itemized on a waiter's tip sheet and signed for by each waiter when he receives his tips at the end of each serving period. This signed form then becomes part of the cashier's closing documentation.

12. Closing procedures should include the following:

    a. The cashier should count the total receipts and prepare his bank for the following day. The remaining cash constitutes his deposit for the shift. This should be counted by denomination (quarters, nickels, single dollars, fives, and so forth) and the amounts entered on a cashier's deposit slip or envelope (see Fig. 13.1).

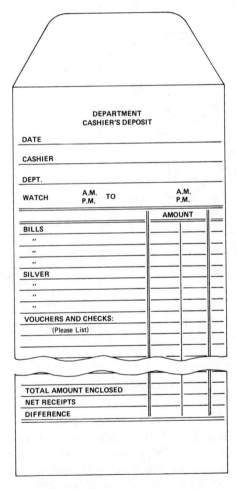

Fig. 13.1. Cashier's deposit envelope.

b. The cashier also prepares a daily report showing the amount of cash and charge sales, tips paid out, and other pertinent data (see Fig. 13.2).

DAILY SALES REPORT			DATE:						PREPARED BY:		
			REGISTER #1		REGISTER #2		REGISTER #3		SALES TX.			TOTAL
			READINGS	TOTAL	READINGS	TOTAL	READINGS	TOTAL	ADJ.			SALES
1	FOOD	END									FOOD	
2		BEG										
3	BEER WINE	END									BEER WINE	
4		BEG										
5	LIQUOR	END									LIQUOR	
6		BEG										
7	TAX	END									TAX	
8		BEG										
9	TIP	END									TIP	
10		BEG										
11												
12												
13	TOTAL SALES										TOTAL SALES	
			CASH A	CASH B	CASH A	CASH B	CASH A	CASH B				
14	CASH	END										
15		BEG										
16	SUB-TOTAL											
17	ADJUSTMENTS											
18	TOTAL											
19	CHARGE	END										
20		BEG										
21	SUB-TOTAL											
22	ADJUSTMENTS											
23	TOTAL										*CHARGE	
24	TIPS PAID										TIPS PAID	
25												
26												
27	ACCT'D FOR										ACCT'D FOR	
28	DEPOSIT										DEPOSIT	
29	(OVER)SHORT										(OV)SHORT	

SUMMARY RESTAURANT				COMMENTS:	* CHARGES SUMMARY	
	LUNCH	DINNER	TOTAL		HOUSE CHRGE	$
FOOD					AMERICAN EXPRESS	
BEER/WINE					DINERS CLUB	
LIQUOR					CARTE BLANCHE	
TOTAL					MASTER CHARGE	
					BANKAMERICARD	
COVERS						
AVG. FOOD						
AVG. BEV.						
COMBINED					TOTAL	

Fig. 13.2. Cashier's report form.

c. The cashier's deposit and report are then turned over to the manager or (in a large operation) to a head cashier or member of the accounting staff. For his own protection, the cashier should have a record book or receive a receipt containing the amount of the deposit, the date, and the signature of the person who received the deposit. If the operation has a safe with a drop slot, the cashier should have a witness when making the drop. This witness and the cashier should then sign the record book.

d. In some operations, the cashier's deposit becomes the bank deposit. In this case, the cashier would also prepare the bank deposit slips. Even if the manager does not choose to go to the bank every day, each day's deposit should be kept separate and intact, amounting to the total day's cash sales (minus any tips paid out). This provides an audit trail for future reference.

13. Register readings should be taken by someone other than the cashier. Registers should not be reset; the readings should continue from one day to the next. The difference between the opening and closing readings should agree with the amount shown on the cashier's daily report. It should be adjusted for any amounts on the cashier's error sheet. If not, the cashier is either "over" or "short."

Security of Cash and Merchandise

There are four classes of thefts.

Thefts by Others

- Robberies

Thefts by Customers

- Short-change artists
- Walkouts
- Counterfeit or altered money
- Credit card fraud
- Bad checks

Thefts by Cashiers

- Shortchanging customers
- Not ringing up exact change sales
- Ringing up sales at less than the full amount, permitting an overage that is subsequently removed from the drawer

Thefts by Waiters

- Not charging for food or drinks served
- Not turning in all funds collected to the cashier
- Overcharging guests and turning in the correct amount
- Pricing checks incorrectly
- Misusing checks or dupes to obtain extra food from the kitchen for himself or his friends

Robberies

The experts are unanimous in their advice in handling robberies. Don't try to be a hero; you may be a dead hero. The Continental Illinois National Bank advises[1]

If You Are Robbed: Do not resist! Money is replaceable; human life is not. Since many robbers are nervous amateurs or desperate drug addicts in need of quick money to support their habit, resistance may lead to injury or death.

To help apprehend and successfully prosecute a robber, victims and other witnesses to the robbery must be able to identify an offender and link him to a criminal act. Remembering the personal characteristics of the robber (Fig. 13.3) as well as the other items listed below will aid in later apprehension, identification, and conviction:

1. Body build (thin, medium, or stocky); height and weight
2. Any readily distinguishable marks, scars, tattoos, or deformities
3. The color and style of the robber's hair, his facial characteristics and complexion, whether he has a beard or mustache, and the color of his eyes
4. Type of clothes the robber was wearing
5. Peculiarities—distinguishable mannerisms, accent, limp, or other distinguishing physical characteristic
6. Type, color, size, and shape of weapon
7. Mode and direction of escape—if by car, get a description of the car, its license number, and, when possible, a description of the driver if the robbery was a two-person job
8. Type of receptacle the money or goods were placed in, i.e., paper bag, cloth bag

Call the police as soon as it is safe. Tell them where the robbery occurred, when it occurred, and the mode and direction of flight. Encourage witnesses to remain and refrain from talking with one another about the crime until the police have arrived. Do not move or even handle any items which the robbers may have touched or disturb any evidence.

You can reduce your chances of being robbed. Question suspicious persons loitering about the premises. Have training sessions with the staff to make them security conscious too. If enough people ask questions, a potential robber may go elsewhere.

Don't keep large amounts of cash on the premises, and don't count money in a public area. Take it to a secure office, away from view. If you have a robbery, don't immediately report the amount taken. A large amount reported in the press may attract more robbers in the future.

---

[1]*Businessman's Guide to Protection Against Crime,* Continental Illinois Bank and Trust Company of Chicago, 1974.

Thefts by Customers

Short-Change Artists

The short-change artist is a professional. He counts on carelessness and inattentiveness by the cashier to pull his act. When the customer pays the waiter, this thief has much less opportunity to rob. However, he may claim to have given the waiter a larger denomination bill than was actually rendered. Waiters should be trained to enter on the check the amount of money received and to verbally acknowledge the amount to the guest.

When customers pay cashiers, it is a different story. Cashiers should be trained to be alert to the short-change artist. Concentration and careful adherence to the correct cashiering procedures are the only way to thwart this individual.

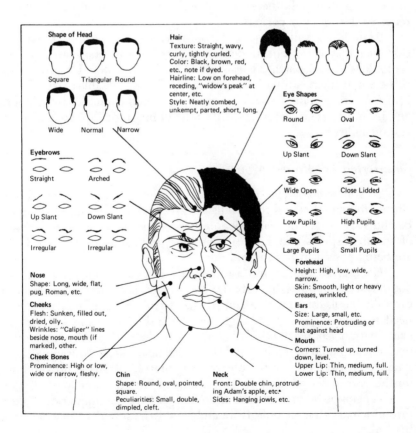

Fig. 13.3. Personal characteristics of a robber.

Walkouts

A walkout is a customer who leaves without paying his check. This type of loss can be reduced by an alert staff. Where customers pay the waiter, it is definitely the responsibility of the service staff to see that all checks are settled. When waiters work in teams, one member should always be on the station, alert to any guests who look like they are going to take a walk. When waiters work singly, it is more difficult to prevent a walkout, but captains and supervisors should always be on the lookout.

Walkouts are more prevalent when customers pay the cashier directly. It becomes quite easy to mingle with a group of people paying at the door and slip out undetected. Under no circumstances should a cashier leave the cash station to chase a walkout. He should call the manager. If the losses from walkouts become significant, it may be a good idea to have a manager stationed near the door during busy periods.

The physical layout of the restaurant may also contribute to walkouts. If there is a secondary exit from the dining room, some means of securing it may be necessary. Also, a second cashier stand may be required during busy periods.

Handling a walkout is touchy. Some walkouts are unintentional; the customer may be absentminded or engaged in conversation. A tactful reminder to the departing guest should be the first step. Usually, this is sufficient. If the customer is out the door, it is not advisable to try to chase him. You are outside of your own premises, and the individual could turn and harm you. The customers still in the dining room are your primary responsibility.

Counterfeit or Altered Money

Anyone who handles cash should be trained to detect counterfeit or altered money. If any of these bills are accepted, the restaurant is stuck. Bad bills are usually of a large denomination, such as $20s and $50s. They often run in spurts, and the local police may put out an alert that bad bills are being passed in the community.

Counterfeit money has a different feel to it. If you get a bill that doesn't seem quite right, especially a large denomination, examine it carefully. Look for tiny blue and red hairs embedded in the paper. You need to have a good strong light on the cashier's station for such an examination. Counterfeit bills will not have these lines. Also, the points on the seal should be distinct and clear with no broken or missing points. Smudged background on the portrait and blurred details or broken lines on the border design are also indications of "funny" money.

A genuine bill may also be altered to raise the denomination. Take a careful look at all large bills, front and back, to be sure that they have not been altered.

Credit Card Fraud

Credit cards are a fact of life these days, and most table service restaurants honor them. When handling a credit card transaction, you should observe the following steps:

1. Check the expiration date to see if the card is still valid.
2. Compare the signature on the charge ticket with that on the card to see if they are the same.
3. Card companies publish lists of stolen, lost, or canceled cards. Check to see if the card is on the current list. If it is and you accept the charge, you can be stuck for the total amount of the bill.
4. Card companies also have a floor limit. All transactions above this amount must be cleared by telephone call with the credit card company, even if the card number is not on the blacklist. The amount of the floor limit varies according to the company and the type of restaurant.
5. If there is any doubt about the validity of the credit card or if it appears to have been altered or defaced, ask for additional identification. Get the customer to sign the guest check and compare signatures.
6. If there is any indication of foul play, detain the customer and call the manager.

Checking lists for a large number of transactions can slow down the cashier considerably. Some credit card companies have available a small computer terminal that will automatically check the validity of the card while imprinting the card voucher.

Bad Checks

Payment by check is not as common in restaurants as payment by credit card. However, many restaurants will accept a check as a last resort to collect from a customer. To reduce the exposure to risk, the Continental Bank advises the following steps in handling a check transaction:[2]

1. Read the check face and back. It should look like a check. Some stores have cashed telephone bills paying the amount due on the bill. Record vouchers or advertising devices also have been presented as bona fide checks and cashed.

---

[2]*Businessman's Guide to Protection Against Crime*, Continental Illinois Bank and Trust Company of Chicago, 1974.

2. A check must be properly made out:
   - If it is a personal check payable to the store or establishment, it should bear the date it is cashed (within two or three days of cashing).
   - The writer's name and address should be imprinted on the face of the check.
   - It should be made out to the store or establishment cashing it.
   - The amount in numbers should be identical to the spelled-out amount.
   - The bank's name and address should be imprinted on the check.
   - The signature of the maker should be legible, as should all writing on the check.
3. The check should not show signs of erasures or alterations; if either is present, the check should not be cashed.
4. Identification should be required. Certain types of identification that are hard to steal or duplicate bear the name and description of the person to whom they are issued, or demonstrate that the individual's credit-worthiness has been previously determined. Only these forms of identification should be used to determine whether to cash a check, but even then it is best to ask for two or three. Examples include a valid driver's license, an employee I.D. card bearing a picture, or a store's own credit card if it has a signature.
   - The description on the identification card ("I.D.") should be carefully checked to make sure that it matches the appearance of the person cashing the check.
   - The signature on the I.D. should be compared with that of the person cashing the check.
   - The name, address, and phone number on the check should match that on the I.D.
   - The type of I.D. presented and the physical description of the person cashing the check should be noted on the back of the check.
   - The check should be re-endorsed in the cashier's presence if there is doubt that the check passer signed the check originally. Often a forger will not be able to spell even the name of the payee or to duplicate the previous endorsement.
   - Remember, check cashing is a courtesy; you have no obligation to cash any check. But keep in mind too that it is an integral and necessary part of the transfer of funds process.

Thefts by Cashiers and Waiters

These types of thefts may victimize the customer as well as the restaurant. Cashier thefts include pocketing the amount of an exact change transaction and destroying the check or ringing up less than the amount of the check and taking the difference. Another type of cashier theft is short-changing the guest. With waiters, theft techniques include swinging checks, that is, using the same check to collect from several customers and only turning in the last collection, or using another customer's check to overcharge a guest and turning in the correct check and amount; altering checks to overcharge the guest and then turning in the correct amount; not charging for certain items in hopes of getting a bigger tip; and (intentionally or unintentionally) pricing or adding incorrectly.

These types of theft can be minimized by the following techniques:

1. The first defense is a good offense. Check carefully the people you hire. Have all cashiers and people handling money bonded. The bonding company's security check is very helpful.
2. Investigate any cashier who works with the drawer open; who works with a note pad with scribbled numbers; or who frequently rings up no sales, voids checks, or splits amounts.
3. Make a policy that no erasures are permitted on checks and that any check on which the amount is changed must be approved by a supervisor.
4. Review the guest checks periodically for indications of erasures, misrings, improper pricing and totaling, or improper or missing validation marks from the cash settlement register.
5. Where counter attendants and bartenders collect their own checks and ring them up, provide a locked drop box with a slot for closed checks and require the server to deposit each check in the box as soon as the transaction is completed.
6. Use spotters from an outside shopper service to check on the waiter and cashier procedures being used.
7. From time to time, pull the cashier's drawer in the middle of service. Have a supervisor step in and cover the station while you and the cashier count the amount collected in the till. Investigate any large overages or shortages in the cash count at that time. Let your cashiers know that you will be doing this as a matter of routine. An honest cashier won't mind.
8. Require that all prices be imprinted on the checks by machine. Do not permit prices to be penciled in on the checks.
9. Account for all missing checks on a daily basis and keep all reserve checks locked up.
10. Provide adding machines and insist that waiters use them to total checks if they are not machine totaled.
11. Consider the use of electronic point-of-sale register equipment.
12. Match up guest checks with the dupes from the kitchen (if they are used) on a test basis.

13. Time stamp checks at the range in the kitchen and at the time of settlement. Spot check how long the check was open. An unreasonable span of time may mean it was used for more than one transaction.

14. Employees with positive attitudes and close identification with their employer seldom steal. Work toward establishing a good morale by paying fair rates and treating the employees as an important part of your team (which, of course, they are).

15. Many young people today do not have the same values toward property that their elders had. Keep especially close tabs on younger employees. Fire anyone caught stealing, regardless of the amount. One bad apple can spoil the bunch. It is not a matter of how much was stolen but the fact that it was stolen. Establish this policy quickly and follow through.

16. Law enforcement agencies encourage managers to prosecute all persons caught stealing (regardless of the amount) as a deterrent to others. If the offender is a young person in his first job, you must follow your own conscience as to whether pressing charges is warranted.

The Cashier and the Public

The cashier who deals directly with the customer is the last person to see the guest before he leaves the restaurant. A guest who has a complaint often won't register it until he has to part with his cash. For this reason, cashiers often hear complaints and should not pass them over lightly. *Never let a dissatisfied guest leave the restaurant.*

At the point of payment, it is too late to correct a problem with the meal or service, but the situation may be saved by offering a future meal, a drink, or bottle of wine, or by deducting something from the check. These gestures must be made by a supervisor or manager, however, and not by a cashier. If a supervisor is not available, or if the guest does not want to wait, the cashier should get his name and telephone number or address so that a call or letter can subsequently be sent. Failing all else, the cashier should note the complaint, apologize graciously, and report it to the supervisor or manager as soon as possible. A delay in correcting a problem could mean that other guests may be dissatisfied.

As with all other front of the house personnel, cashiers need to be well groomed and pleasant mannered. Having a good telephone voice is important since answering the phone is usually part of their duties. Cashiers should also have a good knowledge of the neighborhood and happenings around town since they are apt to be asked questions and directions by departing guests.

Appendix A

Guidelines for a Safety Self-Inspection Program

Why Self-Inspection?

Why is a self-inspection program of importance to a foodservice operator? Both customers and employees are exposed to the accident and health hazards inherent in a foodservice operation. The employee faces all manner of operational hazards during his duty day. Few occupations confront an employee with such a multiplicity of types of hazardous equipment and conditions. The customer also faces hazards to safety when he or she enters the establishment.

The foodservice operator's interest in protecting both customers and employees is not primarily to meet the requirements of the federal Occupational Safety and Health Act or equivalent state regulations, nor to provide evidence to the OSHA inspector on the occasion of his relatively infrequent inspection visits. The operator's obligation to protect both customers and employees is of primary importance! Furthermore, the success, if not the survival, of a foodservice operation depends considerably upon the daily safeness of facilities and operational practices.

Many factors are pertinent to the economics and the practical aspects of achieving an effective, continuing operation. Employee injuries can mean compensation costs and loss of the employee's services. Customer illness or injury can mean claims, law suits, and loss of patronage.

Adapted from *A Safety Self-Inspection Program for Food Service Operators*, National Restaurant Association, Chicago, Illinois, 1974.

The foodservice operator cannot afford to ignore safety in his operation. He must involve himself personally in seeing that employees are properly instructed and supervised; that hazards to health and safety are identified and either controlled or eliminated. A comprehensive and effective self-inspection program is essential to an organized loss control program and will provide the operator with the information that he must have to evaluate the effectiveness of his safety efforts and to indicate to him the weak points which require action on his part.

How Frequently Should Inspections Be Accomplished?

Inspection frequencies should be based on the relative magnitude of hazards to safety and health. Critical points in operational procedures and those inherent in certain types of equipment should be identified, and more frequent inspections of these should be scheduled. However, relatively frequent inspections of the entire operation should be accomplished for the purpose of checking on the adequacy and completeness of supervision and to ensure that *all* areas and activities are being covered to identify and correct deficiencies, and eliminate hazards.

How Should Inspection Check Sheets Be Developed?

Inspection check sheets should be developed by, and for, specific operations or establishments, in order that they will include that which is pertinent to the procedures and equipment types of that operation. Inspection check sheets should be separately accomplished for specific functional areas or procedures. A single all-inclusive self-inspection form is self-defeating, as it will seldom be used.

It is particularly desirable that a foodservice company or operation develop its own self-inspection program and inspection forms to ensure that they are specifically applicable to company policies, practices and procedures and that they are compatible with state and local safety regulations.

The inspection check sheets included in this book are provided for your use and guidance in building a self-inspection program pertinent to your operation. You will find that, when you have discarded those check sheets which do not apply to your operation, you will have a set applicable to your needs.

These sheets are not designed to provide a numerical rating or score. The format is based on their anticipated use as a practical management tool. Thus, they are designed to provide you with an indication that each specific practice or procedure or specific item of equipment or functional area is either satisfactory or unsatisfactory. Space is provided following each item for comments regarding deficiencies noted and corrective action desired. The date column makes possible the recording of when the correction is accomplished.

What Follow-Up Actions Should Be Taken?

The foodservice operator should initiate appropriate action to correct undesirable situations revealed by self-inspections. These unsafe situations should be emphasized during training sessions for employees or through the media of employee bulletins, newsletters and posters.

A file of the self-inspection reports should be maintained to permit management review of (1) the immediate and long-range effectiveness of the self-inspection program, (2) the effectiveness of supervision over operations, (3) the promptness and adequacy of action taken to correct unsatisfactory procedures and conditions, and (4) the subjects requiring training emphasis. The foodservice operator should also compare his inspection reports with those of casualty and fire inspectors and coordinate follow-up action. For helpful guidance on safety, write to the following for a copy of the NRA's catalog of books, bulletins, films and pamphlets:

Educational Materials Center
National Restaurant Association
One IBM Plaza
Chicago, Illinois 60611

Particularly useful will be the publications:

- Your Responsibility for Safety (8-page booklet)
- An Employee Safety Message for Foodservice Operators (safety case histories) (12-page booklet)
- Safety Data Sheet—Kitchen Machines (6-pages)
- Safety Data Sheet—Hand Knives (8-pages)
- Emergency Treatment of Burns (chart)
- Chemical Hazards (chart)
- Pest Prevention (16-page booklet)

Sound-filmstrip programs

- Work Smart—Stay Safe
- The Freeloaders (pest control)

Personal Safeness	Comments on Deficiencies Noted and Action Required	Date Corrected
Are employees with physical limitations doing inappropriate work?		
Are employees wearing suitable, low heeled shoes which minimize slipping or falling?		
Is employee clothing free of raggedness and looseness which could be hazardous around moving equipment?		
Are employees wearing loose or dangling jewelry which could be a hazard near moving equipment or could get into food?		
Are employees observed smoking in unauthorized areas?		
Are employees with long hair wearing adequate hair restraints to prevent risk of entanglement?		
Are employees who are under the influence of drugs or alcohol permitted to work?		

Working Practices	Comments on Deficiencies Noted and Action Required	Date Corrected
Do employees understand the hazards and necessary precautions which apply to the jobs they are doing?		

Are deliberate violations of safety rules
observed?

Are employees observed engaging in
horseplay, teasing or playfully distracting
fellow workers?

Are tray stands, condiment trays, chairs,
mop buckets etc., in aisle-ways or traffic
ways?

Are spills wiped up or swept up
promptly?

Are utensils and other objects picked up
promptly?

Are employees who are doing heavy
lifting, accomplishing it in the proper
manner?

Are employees observed to stand on
boxes, chairs, or other unsafe devices to
perform tasks?

Are employees observed dipping
crushed ice or ice cubes with drinking
glasses?

Is employee observed moving equipment
which is in operation (floor fan, slicer,
etc.)?

Are employees using hand knives
properly and safely?

Working Practices (cont.)	Comments on Deficiencies Noted and Action Required	Date Corrected
Is employee observed to pick up broken glass by hand?		

Floors and Walking Surfaces	Comments on Deficiencies Noted and Action Required	Date Corrected
Are floors clear of debris and obstructions?		
Are floors dry?		
Are floors slippery because of slippery surfaces or slippery wax or polish?		
Are floors (traffic-ways) free from protruding obstacles such as nails, pipe ends, ridges, holes or broken tiles?		
Are floors that are being mopped, blocked off or posted?		
Are floor mats, wooden duck boards, etc., in good repair?		
Where carpeted, are there holes, tears or loose threads which could cause tripping?		

Stairways	Comments on Deficiencies Noted and Action Required	Date Corrected
Are stairs in good repair and solid to the step?		
Are step risers of uniform height?		
Are there loose tread pads, runners, non-skid strips, etc.?		
Are railings in good repair, free of splinters, and solid?		
Is stairway free from any obstacles such as trash, boxes, mops and brooms, etc.?		
Is stairwell provided with adequate natural light or well lit?		
Are steps wet from spilled food or liquid?		
Is the floor at the base of stairs clear, clean, dry and free from holes or other hazards?		

Electrical Connections and Equipment	Comments on Deficiencies Noted and Action Required	Date Corrected
Is electrical equipment properly grounded (especially in areas of wetness or dampness)?		
Are electrical outlets overloaded through use of multiple plugs?		
Are frayed, worn or broken electrical cords observed?		
Are loose or unprotected electrical cords on the floor, especially across trafficways (exposed to tripping and to wheeled traffic)?		
Are electrical cords subject to water and dampness?		
Are there any live but empty light sockets or live but damaged switches?		
Are switches for electrical equipment located so that employees do not have to lean on or against metal equipment to reach them?		
Are electrical switches so located that they can be reached easily in the event of an emergency?		
Are switches guarded to prevent inadvertent or accidental switching on?		

Are electrical contacts, receptacles, etc.
free of grease?

Signs	Comments on Deficiencies Noted and Action Required	Date Corrected

Are danger, caution and safety signs
posted where applicable?

Are emergency exits marked by
illuminated standard signs?

Are signs used to direct attention to
obscure exits?

Are "no smoking" signs posted in trash
storage and other areas where a fire
hazard exists?

Are portable signs used to indicate wet
mopped floor or other temporary
hazard?

Lighting	Comments on Deficiencies Noted and Action Required	Date Corrected

Is all lighting adequate to the location
and purpose?

Is all lighting, especially emergency
lighting, operational?

Lighting (cont.)	Comments on Deficiencies Noted and Action Required	Date Corrected
Is lighting provided and operational at stairs and other hazardous floor points where customers or employees might trip?		

Exits	Comments on Deficiencies Noted and Action Required	Date Corrected
Is every exit in the building clearly marked with standard illuminated sign?		
Are exit lights working properly?		
Is false exit marked "no exit" to avoid confusion, especially in emergencies?		
Are any exits blocked with work tables or other equipment? ·		
Are any exits obstructed inside or outside by carts or dollies, boxes and cartons of supplies or trash and debris?		
If an exit is obscure, is sign indicating location of the exit conspicuously posted?		
Are exit doors provided with panic bars or not locked?		

Fire Protection Equipment	Comments on Deficiencies Noted and Action Required	Date Corrected
Are all portable fire extinguishers properly mounted and in view?		
Are any extinguishers blocked or located in hard to reach locations?		
Do all portable extinguishers carry tags indicating date inspected?		
Have all extinguishers been inspected as required?		
Are any extinguishers empty (unreported discharge)?		
Are any discharged extinguishers where they could be mistakenly grabbed for use?		
Are instructions posted, describing types of portable extinguishers and classes of fires they are intended for?		
Are extinguishers located appropriately for the types of hazard(s) involved?		
Are charts showing fire exit routes and the location of fire fighting equipment prominently posted?		

Fire Protection Equipment (cont.)	Comments on Deficiencies Noted and Action Required	Date Corrected
Are all automatic systems in operating condition?		
Are instructions for reporting a fire and calling the fire department conspicuously posted?		
Are all hydrants, hoses, and fire extinguishing system actuating switches unobstructed, clearly marked and visible?		
Are all traffic-ways, stairwells, storage rooms, utilities rooms, etc., free from flammable trash and debris?		
Are flammable or combustible liquids kept in approved separate storage?		

First-Aid Supplies	Comments on Deficiencies Noted and Action Required	Date Corrected
Is a first-aid kit available for emergency use?		
Have the contents been approved by your company doctor?		
Is its location marked conspicuously?		

Is a list of contents posted on or
adjacent to the kit?

Is there an adequate supply of each of
the kit components?

Are the items that deteriorate replaced at
required intervals?

Is at least one employee on each shift
trained to give first-aid?

Food Holding and Serving Equipment	Comments on Deficiencies Noted and Action Required	Date Corrected
Are counters, steam tables and other serving line equipment free from sharp corners?		
Is all electrical equipment properly grounded?		
Is lighting adequate and appropriately guarded?		
Are microwave ovens in good repair, especially doors and seals?		
Are door seals free from grease?		

Food Holding and Serving Equipment (cont.)	Comments on Deficiencies Noted and Action Required	Date Corrected
Are aisleways and traffic-ways unobstructed?		
Is ice storage protected to prevent accidental presence of foreign objects?		
Is glassware stored above open ice bins or used for dipping ice?		
Are service carts in good repair?		

Dining Area(s)	Comments on Deficiencies Noted and Action Required	Date Corrected
Are service doors adequately marked to insure safe traffic patterns?		
Are tray stands and service carts obstructing passageways?		
Are waiters, waitresses or busboys overloading trays?		
Is floor free from food spillage, silverware, broken glassware, loose mats, torn carpets or other hazards?		

Are broken or wobbly chairs or unsteady
tables in use?

Are chairs free from splinters and metal
burrs?

Is chipped or cracked glassware
or dishware in use?

Are customers guarded from hot food
holding equipment?

Customer Rest Rooms	Comments on Deficiencies Noted and Action Required	Date Corrected
Is floor in restroom clean and free from hazardous wetness or soap accumulation?		
Are safe receptacles provided for cigarette butts?		
Is restroom free of trash and debris?		
Are lights and electrical equipment operating satisfactorily?		
Is all furniture and equipment in good repair?		

Your Safety Program	Comments on Deficiencies Noted and Action Required	Date Corrected
Do your employees understand the basic principles of safety and the company's safety policy?		
Do they know the hazards associated with their duties and related equipment?		
Are accidents and near accidents promptly reported and recorded for management action?		
Do employees promptly report all injuries?		
Are employees instructed, counselled and reminded thru: Safety meetings or on the job safety training, safety newsletters or safety items in company periodicals, and special posters, bulletins or signs?		
Is an active safety committee concerning itself about safety in your operation?		
Do you have a recognition or award program for good employee or departmental safety records?		
Are employees encouraged to report hazards and suggest safety improvements?		

Appendix B

Guidelines for a Sanitation and Safe Food Handling Self-Inspection Program

Why Self-Inspection?

The initial impression a customer receives of your establishment determines to a considerable degree the extent of his future patronage. Very important to you is what the customer sees during his visit ... hopefully, a bright, clean and attractive place in which to dine. More important to him is what your customer, for the most part, does not see— the personal hygiene practices of your employees; the manner in which food is handled during storage, preparation and serving; and the manner in which equipment and utensils are cleaned and sanitized.

The extent to which your employees practice good personal hygiene, prepare and serve food in a safe manner and maintain equipment and utensils in a clean and sanitary condition, measures the extent to which you protect your customers from contaminated food and possible foodborne illness.

Adapted from *A Self-Inspection Program for Food Service Operators on Sanitation and Safe Food Handling*, National Restaurant Association, Chicago, Illinois, 1973.

The effective protection of your customer can best be achieved by a continuing program of self-inspection of both facilities and practices. This self-inspection program is not for the purpose of preparing for a regulatory agency inspection, but rather to provide a continual check on the adequacy and completeness of supervision and on the safety of all areas and activities of your operations. Inspections should be conducted as often as necessary to assure that deficiencies are discovered and corrected promptly.

The NRA booklet provides sample check lists for use in a self-inspection program. These include points covered in most public health departments and other enforcement agencies, as well as what the NRA calls "customer concerns." These sample forms must be modified to fit your particular restaurant operation and to meet your local health department requirements.

These sheets are not designed to provide for a numerical rating or score. Rather, they are designed to provide you with an indication that a given practice or facility is either satisfactory or unsatisfactory. Space is provided for the entry of pertinent comments concerning the specifics of deficiencies noted and corrective action required. The date column makes possible the recording of the date when correction is accomplished.

What Follow-Up Actions Should Be Taken?

You will want to initiate appropriate action to correct undesirable situations which your self-inspections may reveal and you will, no doubt, include mention of some of them during training sessions for employees or through the media of your employee bulletins, newsletters and posters.

It would be useful for you to maintain a file of your self-inspection reports to permit your management review of (1) the immediate and long-range effectiveness of your self-inspection program, of (2) the effectiveness of supervision over your operations and of (3) the promptness and adequacy of action to correct unsatisfactory procedures and conditions.

What Benefits May Accrue to the Foodservice Operation When Inspection and Follow-Up Actions Are Recorded?

When a file is maintained on the self-inspections accomplished and on follow-up actions taken to correct undesirable situations and to bring deficient procedures and conditions to the attention of your employees, a number of benefits can result:

1. When copies are furnished to your regulatory department or shown to your regulatory department's sanitation inspector, they will know

the extent of your interest in maintaining a safe operation and of your continuing program to identify and correct unsafe conditions. This could lead to a reduction in the number of official inspections made of your establishment, as the regulatory department turns its attention to problem establishments. Regulatory officials will also be able to recognize conditions or situations with which you are having difficulty and, in many cases, will be able to assist you in resolving them.

2. Your self-inspection records will be useful as evidence of your interest and effectiveness in maintaining a safe and sanitary operation in case you are confronted by representatives from the news media or consumer groups.

3. Your continuing review of both inspection results and follow-up action will, undoubtedly, protect you from law suits and claims because of action you have taken to reduce or eliminate illness causes. For helpful guidance on sanitation and safe food handling, write to the following for a copy of the NRA's catalog of books, bulletins, films and pamphlets:

> Educational Materials Center
> National Restaurant Association
> One IBM Plaza, Chicago, Illionis 60611

Particularly useful will be the publications:

- Foodborne Illnesses (reference chart)
- Hot Facts About Food Protection (leaflet)
- Cold Facts About Food Protection (leaflet)
- Temperatures for Food Safeness (chart)
- Don't Serve Illness to our Customers (chart)
- Pest Prevention (16 page technical bulletin)

Sound-filmstrip programs:

- Protecting the Public
- The Unwanted Four
- The Freeloaders

Personal Safeness (Infections and Illness, Hygiene, and Grooming)	Comments on Deficiencies Noted and Action Required	Date Corrected
Do any food handlers have infected burns, cuts, boils?		
Do any food handlers have acute respiratory illness?		
Do any food handlers have infections or contagious illness transmittable through foods?		
Are food handlers wearing clean outer garments?		
Are food handlers free of body odors?		
Are food handlers' hands clean— washed at start of work day and as frequently as necessary?		
Are food handlers wearing hats, caps or hairnets or other effective hair restraints?		
Are food handlers observed smoking or eating in food preparation or serving areas?		
Are fingernails of food handlers short and clean?		

Are food servers seen to cough in
hands?

Are food handlers wearing rings (other
than plain band), dangling bracelets,
wristwatches, etc. while preparing or
handling food?

Have all employees been instructed on
minimum sanitation and food protection
requirements?

Food Handling Practices	Comments on Deficiencies Noted and Action Required	Date Corrected

Are hands being used to pick up rolls,
bread, butter pats, ice, or other food to
be served?

Are waitresses or busboys handling place
settings and serving food without
washing hands after wiping tables and
bussing soiled dishes?

Are food servers touching food contact
surfaces of plates, tumblers, cups and
silverware when setting table or serving
customer?

Is floor being swept while food is
exposed, being served or when
customers are eating?

Dining Room and Serving Area	Comments on Deficiencies Noted and Action Required	Date Corrected

Is dining area, including floor, tables and
chairs, clean and dry?

Dining Room and Serving Area (cont.)	Comments on Deficiencies Noted and Action Required	Date Corrected
Is tableware clean and sanitized and stored in a manner to prevent splash and contamination?		
Are single service items stored and dispensed in a sanitary manner?		
Are single service items disposed of after single use?		
Are clean and sanitary cloths used for wiping dining tables and chairs?		
Are silverware and serving utensils stored and presented in a manner to prevent contamination and to insure their being picked up by the handles?		

Refrigerator Storage	Comments on Deficiencies Noted and Action Required	Date Corrected
Are all refrigerators operating?		
Are refrigerators equipped with accurate thermometers?		
Are refrigerators maintaining potentially hazardous foods at temperatures of 45° F or lower?		
Are refrigerators clean and free from mold and objectionable odors?		

Rest Rooms (Customer Concerns)	Comments on Deficiencies Noted and Action Required	Date Corrected
Are customer restrooms clean, dry, light, well ventilated and free of odor?		
Is all sanitary equipment operating satisfactorily?		
Is there a satisfactory supply of soap, towels and tissue?		
Are waste containers covered and kept clean?		
Are waste containers emptied frequently?		
Is there adequate hot and cold water?		
Are all drains operating in a satisfactory manner?		
Is there any sign of rodents or insects?		
Are toilet doors self-closing and in good working order?		

Entrance and Foyer or Waiting Room (Customer Concerns)	Comments on Deficiencies Noted and Action Required	Date Corrected
Is the entryway and waiting room clean and attractive?		
Is it free from litter?		
Are chairs and benches clean and lamps and fixtures clean and free from dust?		
Are posters and printed materials clean and neatly racked or posted?		
Does the customer's first view of your establishment convey the image of cleanliness and freshness?		

General Cleanliness of Dining Area (Customer Concerns)	Comments on Deficiencies Noted and Action Required	Date Corrected
Is the floor dirty, dingy or littered, particularly with food particles and napkins?		
Are tables streaked and condiments dirty?		
Are there crumbs, spilled liquid on chairs or benches?		

Are menus food-marked or worn and
dirty?

Are table linens food-marked? Are they
tattered or torn?

Is tableware cracked, chipped, streaked
or food-soiled?

Is silverware thumb-marked, dingy,
spotted or food-soiled?

Are soiled dish trays left near customer
tables?

A point of safety—are insect sprays
being used when food is exposed or
customers are present?

Cleanliness of Service Personnel (Customer Concerns)	Comments on Deficiencies Noted and Action Required	Date Corrected

Are waitress uniforms crumpled or
soiled?

Are waitresses using strong or offensive
perfume or smelling of body odor?

Are servers sniffing, coughing or
rubbing or wiping nose?

Cleanliness of Service Personnel (Customer Concerns) (cont.)	Comments on Deficiencies Noted and Action Required	Date Corrected
Do servers handle drinking glasses by their tops or silverware by their blades, tines or bowls?		
Are waitresses wearing shaggy hair-dos and wigs?		
Do cooks and servers smoke in view of customers?		
Do servers handle rolls, butter, ice, etc. by hand in filling dishes and water glasses?		
Do cooks, servers or busboys scratch head, face or body in view of customers?		
Does server touch food with thumb or fingers when serving plated food?		

Sensory Factors (Customer Concerns)	Comments on Deficiencies Noted and Action Required	Date Corrected
Is dining area too hot or cold for customer comfort?		
Is heat and steam from serving line unpleasant for customers (and the servers)?		

Is light in dining area too bright and
glary?

Is light too dim, that customer has
difficulty seeing the menu and his food
and tableware?

Is clatter of dish and warewashing
offensive to the customer?

Is loudness of waitresses, cooks or
busboys offensive and distracting to the
customer?

Are busboys too noisy in handling
removal of soiled tableware?

Does odor of the kitchen greet the
customer as he enters the dining room?

Are strong odors of odiferous food types
noticeable in the dining area or
externally?

Is there an "old grease" odor in the
dining room or as exhausted to the
street or parking area?

Is spoiled food disposed of promptly to
prevent obnoxious odor?

Appendix C

Training Manual

Following is a portion of the training manual for the Corner, a restaurant in New York's World Trade Center (used by permission of Inhilco).

Welcome to the Corner!

Our restaurant, like all of the other food facilities in the World Trade Center, is operated by Inhilco, Inc. Our company is a subsidiary of Hilton International, which, in turn, is owned by TWA.

The Corner is similar in style to a brasserie (an informal French restaurant), but uses American-style menus. The Corner is open from 7 am to 8 pm. The breakfast menu is in use until 11:30 am, at which time the Corner switches to its lunch menu, which is in use for the rest of the day. The assistant manager seats your guests and gives them the menus. You serve them and present the check. The cashier receives the cash. The busboys clean and restock your stations every evening and continually replenish your supplies, clear bus pans and help with the clearing and resetting of tables and counters. Our clientele is largely made up of the business people who work at the World Trade Center. These guests are busy people with limited time for meals.

In order to accommodate our guests, the service in the Corner is fast, yet efficient and excellent in quality. We expect you to meet our high standards of job performance and, above all, to always be courteous to our guests.

This manual explains all of the tasks you will be required to do. By studying it, and practicing the tasks, you will acquire the skills necessary to perform your job excellently. You will become a professional waitress.

Appearance, Conduct, and Other House Rules

At the Corner, you are visible to the guests at all times. Customers notice the way you look and act, and they form an impression of you. The opinion a customer forms of the Corner is strongly influenced by his opinion of you. By abiding by our policies of appearance and conduct, indicated below, you will leave a lasting positive impression on your customers and you will build a fine reputation for the Corner.

Appearance

You should be impeccably groomed at all times. Your hair should be neat and styled. Pull it back, if it is long, and do not let it fly around, as this is unsanitary. In order to look your best, we require that you wear lipstick, powder and eye make-up, lightly applied and refreshed before each meal. Jewelry should be kept to a minimum. Only small rings, small earrings and a wrist watch are permitted. Bracelets, necklaces, dangling earrings or other large jewelry are not allowed. Because we do not want the customer to smell perfume when he is served his food, you are not allowed to wear any fragrances.

The company will provide you with a uniform, however, it is your responsibility to keep it clean and in good condition. Be sure that it fits you properly. In addition to your uniform, you will have to wear a black, conservative shoe, with closed toe and heel, and neutral, sheer stockings, free of runs. The shoes and stockings are not provided by the company.

Conduct

You should always act like you are a professional: alert, efficient, and attentive to your work. Some simple guidelines, listed below, will help you acquire the professional manner which will distinguish you in the eyes of your guests.

1. Be aware of *what* you say. Do not discuss personal matters and do not talk shop within earshot of the customers.
2. Be aware of the *volume* of your voice. Develop the habit of talking in a whisper to fellow employees. Do not shout across the slide to cooks; call the manager if you have any problem. Direct your busboy unobtrusively.
3. Be aware of your posture. Stand straight and look alert. Do not slouch, lean on slide, or place checks on table while writing. Place arms at your side; do not stand with arms folded or hands in pockets. Bend down elegantly.
4. Show the customer that your attention is on your work. Do not stand around in groups, socializing with fellow employees.
5. Confine your eating, drinking, smoking, reading, chewing gum, sitting, etc. to T4 during your breaks. This conduct is not allowed on the floor.

6. Count tips during your breaks or after work—not while you are on the floor.
7. Arrange your hair and apply make-up before you begin your shift—not while working.

Employee Meals

You are allowed two free meals on your eight hour shift. You may eat on your break or before or after work, but never during work. Eat only in the employee eating area (at T4).

Since you will be eating in the front-of-the-house, your professional conduct must be maintained during your breaks. Avoid acting in a manner that suggests a party is going on. Sit in small groups, with both feet under the table, so customers can walk through the aisle easily.

Select your meal from the list of foods allowed to employees. Then list on a meal check *every* item you have selected. Have the manager or assistant manager sign your meal check. When this is done, you may order your food from the cook. (Note: list every item on the meal check, regardless of whether the cook prepares it or you get it yourself. This is important in calculating our food cost accurately.)

Attendance/Lateness

It is absolutely essential to the smooth operation of the Corner that everyone be punctual and have excellent attendance. This is an important requirement of your job. If an emergency or unusual circumstance compels you to be absent or late, notify the manager as far in advance as possible, so arrangements can be made to find a replacement.

Time Cards

Punch your time card at the start and again at the end of your shift. Change clothing before punching in and after punching out. Have a manager initial your time card after you punch out.

Lockers

You will have the use of a personal locker while you are employed here. There is a fee of $2 for the key.

Phone Calls

You are not allowed to make or receive personal phone calls during working hours, except in cases of emergency.

Friends/Visitors

You may not receive friends or visitors in the restaurant during working hours or during your breaks.

Personnel Office

If you feel you have a problem you would like to discuss with Personnel, go to the office or phone for an appointment.

Work Schedule

Stations are rotated on a weekly basis. The schedule is posted two weeks in advance.

How to Serve the Customer

Our customers are the most important part of our business. Their patronage of our stores makes possible the livelihood of every one of us. The sole purpose of all of our work is to serve them.

It is *you* who have direct contact with our guests. This is why the responsibility of making customers for the Corner and keeping them satisfied largely rests on your shoulders.

In addition, fine service will be of personal benefit to you, because it results in higher tips.

Sample Task Description—How to Use the Espresso Coffee Machine

The following is an example of a task description which may be included in a training manual.

Directions for Making One Cup of Espresso

1. Fill strainer with 1 level spoonful of espresso (use brown measuring spoon). Do not pack down.
2. Insert strainer into machine and lock.
3. Set dial at left to "4".
4. Place cup under spigot.
5. Slide small brown handle to left to start machine.
6. Handle will release when coffee is ready to serve.
7. Remove strainer and dump used grounds; rinse.

Directions for Making Two Cups of Espresso

Same as above except

1. Use 1 heaping spoonful—again, do not pack down.
2. Set dial to "6".
3. Use double strainer handle.

Directions for Making Cappuccino

Make espresso as usual and top it with steamed milkfoam.

To make steamed milkfoam, use a large pitcher and pour milk in—a few ounces only—pull out steam nozzle at extreme left or right and place pitcher under as deep as possible. Turn valve above all the way open carefully and work nozzle around until you can see it frothing well. Espresso should be placed in a soup mug and served with milk froth and rest of ingredients. It is best not to pour milk froth through spout but from the top.

Directions for Raising Water to Maximum Level

In the morning, the water level of the espresso machine is checked to be sure it is maximum. You should not make coffee unless the water level is maximum. If the water falls below that level, fill to maximum as follows:

- Press red button on right of front. This starts the pump.
- Turn brown lever to the left until water reaches maximum. Look at the water level while you are adjusting it, so you do not exceed the maximum.
- Release lever and button.

Appendix D

References

Service

Axler, Bruce. *Focus on: Showmanship in the Dining Room.*
Indianapolis, Indiana: ITT Educational Publishing Co., 1974.
———. *Focus on: Tableservice Techniques.* Indianapolis, Indiana:
ITT Educational Publishing Co., 1974.
Cornell University, School of Hotel Administration. *Essentials
of Good Table Service.* Ithaca, N.Y.: 1971.
Dahmer, Sondra, and Kahl, Kurt. *The Waiter and Waitress Training
Manual.* Boston, Mass.: CBI Publishing, 1974.
Finance, Charles. *Buffet Catering* Rochelle Park, N.J.: Hayden
Book Co., 1975.
Forster, August. *American Culinary Art.* Rochelle Park, N.J.:
Hayden Book Co., 1958.
Fuller, John. *Gueridon and Lamp Cookery.* Rochelle Park, N.J.:
Hayden Book Co., 1964.
Gilbert, Edith. *Let's Set the Table.* 510 Michigan Avenue,
Charlevoix, Michigan: Jet'Iquette, 1972.
Hirsch, Sylvia. *The Art of Table Setting and Flower Arrangement.*
New York, N.Y.: Thomas Y. Crowell Co., 1967.
Huebener, Paul O. *Gourmet Table Service: A Professional Guide.*
Rochelle Park, N.J.: Hayden Book Co., 1968.
Lang, Howard F. *Catering.* Rochelle Park, N.J.: Hayden Book
Co., 1975.
Lehrman, Lewis. *Dining Room Service.* Indianapolis, Indiana:
ITT Educational Publishing Co., 1971.
Mulcahy, Cherie, and Corbin, Robert. *It Pays to Be a Pro.*
3147 Far Hills Avenue, Kettering, Ohio: Foodcraft
Management Corp., 1971.
———. *Today's Busboy.* New York, N.Y.: Chain Store Age Books, 1971.
———. *Today's Cocktail Waitress.* New York, N.Y.: Chain Store
Age Books, 1974.
———. *Today's Waitress.* New York, N.Y.: Chain Store Age Books,
1971.

Waldner, George K., and Mitterhauser. *Professional Chef's Book of Buffets*. Boston, Mass.: Cahners Books, 1968.
Weiss, Edith, and Weiss, Hal. *Catering Handbook*. Rochelle Park, N.J.: Hayden Book Co., 1971.

Food

Hering, Richard. *Hering's Dictionary of Classical and Modern Cookery*. New York City: Radio City Book Store.
Saulnier, Louis. *Le Repertoiure de la Cuisine*. New York City: Radio City Book Store.
Simon, Andre L., and How, Robin. *Dictionary of Gastronomy*. New York: McGraw-Hill Book Company, 1970.

Beverage

Grossman, Harold J. *Grossman's Guide to Wines, Spirits, and Beers*. New York, N.Y.: Charles Scribner's Sons, 1974.
Haszonics, Joseph, and Barratt, Stuart. *Wine Merchandising*. Rochelle Park, N.J.: Hayden Book Company, 1963.
Lichine, Alexis. *New Encyclopedia of Wines and Spirits*. New York, N.Y.: Alfred A. Knopf, 1974.

Safety and Sanitation

National Restaurant Association. *OSHA: A Technical Bulletin about the Occupational Safety and Health Act*. Chicago: NRA.
———. *A Safety Self-Inspection Program for Food Service Operators*. Chicago: NRA, 1973.
———. *A Self-Inspection Sanitation Program for Food Service Operators*. Chicago: NRA, 1973.

General Restaurant Management

Green, Eric F.; Drake, Galen G.; and Sweeney, F. Jerome. *Profitable Food and Beverage Management: Operations* and *Profitable Food and Beverage Management: Planning*. Rochelle Park, N.J.: Hayden Book Company, Inc., 1978.

Index